Travails Abroad
A MEMOIR OF DISASTERS

by

Bill Nesbitt

Printed and bound in England by www.printondemand-worldwide.com

http://www.fast-print.net/bookshop

TRAVAILS ABROAD: A MEMOIR OF DISASTERS
Copyright © Bill Nesbitt 2017

A catalogue record for this book is available from the British Library

ISBN 978-178456-454-4

First published 2017 by
FASTPRINT PUBLISHING
Peterborough, England.

For

Jen', Roger

Marian and Laurie

who survived…

About the Author

As an author and writer, Bill is probably better known, under his byline of Seàn Collins, for his books set in the shadowy world of international intelligence. He has been contributing, under several bylines, to international magazines and press for four decades. As a travel writer, author, critic and publisher, Bill has travelled extensively, from Taipei and Tahiti to Berlin and Bora Bora.

In *Travails Abroad*, he recounts his travels, taking a retrospective look at the embarrassing dilemmas and outright disasters which have befallen him during his career – from being glued to a jeep in Tahiti to being up to his waist in pebble 'quicksand' on a Turkish beach.

Bill admits that potential travellers reading of his experiences could be forgiven for deciding to stay at home...

Travail (traeverl) literary n. l.

'a painful or excessive labour or exertion.'

'The world is a book, and those who do not
travel read only a page.'

St. Augustine

Contents

Foreword

'I nto every life, a little rain must fall.' In this instance, it was torrential.

This memoir covers forty years of travel as author, writer and critic. Experiences I would rather forget include being locked in the stygian darkness of a railway carriage in a Bavarian siding; of trying to catch a hound which – while I was trying to mend a puncture – ran off with the tyre iron into the dense fog on the summit of a Portuguese mountain, and trying to attract the attention of the staff of a Berlin coffee shop to the fact my wife was on fire.

Obviously, not all my travails are included in this volume. It would be too heavy to carry.

All the disasters in this book are true – I have witnesses. Only some names have been changed, to avoid embarrassment. I trust the disasters I endured may appeal to the reader's sense of humour – and sympathy. They certainly didn't appeal to mine at the time.

Bill Nesbitt

Chapter One
Wine Bottles and Brass Bands

M y first ever sojourn into (West) Germany was on a school trip in the mid-sixties. We stayed in local houses with German families in the small village of Sexau in the Black Forest. The Headmaster, his wife and the History Master stayed at the only inn in the village, into which we were allowed for dinner each evening.

One of my fondest memories involved the Headmaster's wife. I found her in the gästhaus, leaning forward with her forehead on an ice-cold stone pillar. I tapped her gently on the shoulder.

"Heavy night?"

"Beer and schnapps," she moaned, returning to the pillar.

Our stay in the Black Forest – in reality, a heavily wooded range of mountains – was designed to broaden our horizons, culturally and linguistically. In my book, I thought this was a little overambitious.

Nevertheless, the Headmaster did his best to add to our experiences with visits to Freiburg, the Black Forest capital; Germany's highest waterfall at Triberg, the falls at Schaffhausen – which always remind me of the final battle between Sherlock Holmes and Moriarty at the 'Reichenbach Falls'; the Schauinsland, the Feldberg, the highest peak of the Black Forest, and Bodensee, better known as Lake Constance, bordered by Germany, Switzerland and Austria.

At Donaueschingen, we were instructed to be impressed that the puddle surrounded by balustrades, would become the mighty River Danube. The 6th Form appreciated the Danube from behind the nearest building with a packet of Gold Leaf cigarettes, then the extortionate price of eight new pence for twenty in decimal currency.

The Head Boy and Senior Prefects were summoned by the Headmaster to a council of war. This always spelled trouble. Evidently, pupils had been seen around the village after the 9.00pm curfew. We Prefects did not find this particularly surprizing: we were an all boy trip and there were girls in the village. In pairs, we were ordered to take up stations at each end of the village and in the centre. Any boys caught breaking the curfew were to be reported to the Headmaster.

The 'proverbial' hit the fan the following morning.

"As Prefects, you had my trust. This was obviously misplaced." He paused, and looked at each of us, stood to attention, in turn.

"I now find that your idea of imposing the curfew was to do so from the inside of the bar at the edge of the village, drinking beer!"

A voice behind me tried to justify our actions, explaining that we had thought it logical to wait inside the bar, in order to catch them as they came in. I honestly thought the Headmaster was about to become apoplectic.

"From this moment, you are *all* banned from any establishment serving alcohol, for the duration of this trip. Anyone caught breaking this ban will be dealt with severely. Obviously, I would have been better served by setting the pupils to watch the Prefects."

In retrospect, he was probably right.

★ ★ ★ ★

Some years later, I tried to persuade my mother to join me on a trip to Heidelberg. I ran into a problem – it was in Germany. I should have foreseen this, given what had happened when I brought a German girl around for coffee. Mother asked where she was from.

"Hanover," she replied.

"Oh, we flattened that!"

End of relationship with German girl.

It was only when I convinced her that the wartime German bombing raids which had followed her to Portsmouth, Liverpool, Manchester, Plymouth, Birmingham, Coventry and London, did *not* prove Adolf Hitler had singled her out as a major target, that she agreed to join me.

Heidelberg – the Romantic City. Twinned with Cambridge, and home to Germany's oldest university, founded in 1386. The town was placed firmly on the map in 1907, with the discovery of 'the Heidelberg Man', the jawbone of a Neolithic inhabitant. In the 18ᵗʰ Century, Heidelberg had been rebuilt in the fashionable Baroque style. One might say its architecture, particularly from the Renaissance period, was its saviour. During the Second World War, a decision was taken by the Allies not to bomb the town due to its high number of historic buildings and churches.

Heidelberg's reputation as the most romantic town in Germany gave rise to the Heine poem *'I have lost my heart in Heidelberg',* and Romberg's operetta *'The Student Prince.'*

The problems began even before we left Victoria Station. Mother decided she would like a ham sandwich and a cup of tea.

"Two ham sandwiches, one tea, one coffee, please."

This was several years before the rules of hygiene demanded tongs.

At this juncture, I should point out that my mother suffered from terminal racism. In the sixties, immigrants to the UK had mainly come from the West Indies. It was common practise for boarding houses to hang a sign saying 'No gypsies, no Irish and no blacks'. Then, as now, the most vocal racists were those who had little or no contact with the immigrants.

The extremely large, black Jamaican lady leaned under the glass counter and placed the ham sandwiches on plates. Mother's reaction could be heard throughout the Station.

"I'm not eating those – you can't tell if her hands are clean or dirty!"

I was busy, desperately trying to find a crack in the floor.

In Heidelberg, I was lured into a false sense of security. Mother actually seemed to be enjoying the romance of the town. I had put together an itinerary which would make the most of our time there.

The heart of Heidelberg is the *Altstadt,* the Old Town, with everywhere to visit being within walking distance. We began on the Neckarstaden, and the Old Bridge. The 1780's bridge, with its distinctive onion-domed towers, had been the original gate to the town, spanning the River Neckar. On the opposite bank of the river, the Philosopher's Way looked down over the red-stoned castle and the Old Town. For centuries, University professors and philosophers had strolled along its paths, discussing and arguing great academic, often world-changing theories and advanced ideas.

Over the next several days, I shepherded mother around Heidelberg, endeavouring to avoid confrontations. I was beginning to feel like a 'minder'. She had cast her critical eye over the red-stoned castle and its illumination reflected in the River Neckar by night; the old University and Students Prison; the *Kornmarkt* with the Church of the Holy Ghost, and a tram to the Karlstor, the 1781 triumphal arch in honour of the Prince Elector Karl Theodor, and marking the eastern boundary of the town.

Our next stop was entirely deliberate.

If visiting mother at 9.00am in the morning, you would be asked if you would like a drink. She did not mean tea or coffee. A short walk from Karlstor towards the *Altstadt*, was our destination: the *Röter Ochsen*, the favoured watering hole of the University's students since 1703. As we entered, we stepped into a bygone age. Every inch of its walls and ceiling were covered with antique-framed sepia and black-and-white photographs of student classes past; their distinctive, coloured pill-box caps denoting their house loyalties. Every heavy wooden table and chair was covered with student's names and years. One of the University's traditions was that of duelling. No student was considered to have truly graduated until he could sport a sabre scar on his cheek.

I suggested lunch.

"Okay, first impressions?" I turned to Mother.

"Bit cluttered isn't it? Looks like a saleroom."

I found a table and ordered drinks and a menu. I suggested she try the locally-brewed Heidelberger beer. She was not impressed. I ran through the menu, as Mother admitted she could not read German, and had no intention of learning to do so.

"I suggest we do a 'When in Rome' lunch of what the German's are famous for – their sausages. You've a choice of bratwürst, bierwürst, weißwürst-" that was as far as I got.

"We're not in Rome. I'll have the soup."

This was beginning to remind me of one night in Tübingen in the Schwäbian Alb. I had been giving a guest lecture at the University and retired to an inn popular with the students. The problem began when the German student arrived. Pete, a cockney by birth, greeted him with "Grüss Gott. It's Herman the German."

Herman said nothing.

"Where have you been tonight?" Pete persisted.

"Das *kino*."

"So, the cinema, huh? War film, was it?"

"No! I don't wish to talk about the war," Herman pleaded.

Pete picked up his beer glass.

"Nah – neither would we if we'd lost twice…"

That was when the Third World War broke out. It was broken up, eventually, by the *polizei*. I skipped dinner that night due to a severely swollen lip.

Mother appeared to be enjoying her *gülaschsuppe* – really more of a spicy beef stew – served with 'black bread'.

"What's the matter with white bread?" It was a rhetorical question.

I had corresponded with a German pen pal, Kürt, since my schooldays. I contacted him and suggested we meet for lunch at the *Haus zum Ritter*. Built in 1592 by a wealthy cloth merchant, its red sandstone façade denoted its status as Heidelberg's only Renaissance building to have survived The War of Succession.

Kürt and I agreed to split the bill.

He arrived with his girlfriend, Monica, and, introductions over, we took our table for lunch. I noted they chose the most expensive dishes on the menu, with wine to match. As we ordered coffee, Kürt and Monica rose.

"Excuse us – we won't be a minute."

They disappeared in the direction of the toilets.

"They won't be back," pronounced Mother. "You're an idiot."

Fifteen minutes later, with two cold coffees on the table, I attempted to placate Mother by saying "They're probably waiting for us outside."

She snorted.

As I rose from the table, I found my way blocked by the waiter and his burly friend.

"You intend to settle the bill sir, yes?"

"I'm looking for my friends who were at our table," I explained.

"They have left sir. They said you would be settling the bill."

I hated it when Mother was right.

On the final day of the trip, we were sat on a bench in the *Bismarckplatz,* when I just had to ask.

"Mother, was there *anything* in Germany you liked?"

"Yes – the roadworks." She pointed over to the tram station.

I looked.

"There is no roadworks."

Exactly," she nodded vigorously, "they were tearing up the track this morning, and by this afternoon they'd laid new track – and resurfaced the road. You wouldn't see that in England."

Thank God for German efficiency.

Leaving Mother in the square, I went to buy two coffees. I should have known better than to leave her to her own devices. As I stood at the counter, I heard the extremely loud brass band.

"Some kind of festival?" I asked the young guy behind the counter.

"*Nein!*" He spat on the floor. "It is the Neo-Nazi Party."

I stopped smiling. The youth behind the counter shouted after me.

"Your coffees!"

I was too late – she was nowhere in sight.

I ran in the direction of the disappearing rally. Then I caught sight of her, marching merrily along behind the band, in perfect step with the Neo-Nazi supporters. Forcing my way through a watching crowd, I grabbed Mother by the arm, dragging her from the line.

"What the hell do you think you're doing?" I demanded.

"Having a nice time –" she scowled, "or, at least, I was until you ruined it – you know I love a good brass band."

"Mother, you're marching in a New Nazi Party rally."

"What? Why didn't you tell me?"

I should have known it would be my fault.

Dragging her away by the arm, she screamed abuse over her shoulder at the supporters she had been marching with a moment before.

But Heidelberg had spun its magical spell. Every year until her death, she returned to Germany on holiday.

Heidelberg has that effect.

★ ★ ★ ★

A decade later, I happened to again be in Heidelberg staying at one of its leading hotels. Night had fallen and the *Altstadt* was a sea of lights reflected in the river. Disliking hotel prices, I had picked up some wine earlier in the day. It was then I discovered the minibar did not include a corkscrew. In reception, I asked the night manager if he could possibly find me one.

Five minutes passed. Five became ten. Although extremely patient, I was also extremely thirsty. Everyone has their limit. I decided to push the cork back into the bottle.

Bad move.

The bottle went off like Mount Etna, whilst doing a reasonable impression of the fountains at the Palace of Versailles. Unfortunately, the majority of the red wine soaked the reception desk, all the paperwork and books thereon, and the hotel computer. I did what anyone with an IQ would do in this situation – I ran.

Five minutes later, my room telephone rang. Predictably, it was the night manager. He was not a happy man. I held the phone at arm's length as it spewed forth a string of expletives. Finally, I put the phone to my ear and said the only thing I could think of at short notice:

"I'm sorry – I don't understand German…"

Chapter Two
The Frogs of France

I n retrospect, the whole thing can be blamed on an acute attack of professional ethics, leading to a near divorce on the grounds of marital incompetence. It had begun with a commission to write a feature on family holidays. This seemed logical, as I had recently married (first wife: 'the Model'), inheriting three stepdaughters, aged eight, seven and five. My choice was a villa in the Algarve, with pool and maid service, or a camping holiday in the south of France. Based on the premise that families with young children would find a camping holiday the more affordable of the two, I plumped for the Côte D' Azur.

Wrong choice.

Armed with an *attestation* carrying the impressive signature of the *Représentatant Genéral du Secrétariat l'Stat au Tourisme,* assorted guides and a dictionary, we left Victoria on the first stage of a thousand-kilometre journey – by coach.

Never again.

By the time we reached the outskirts of Paris, it was evident that it would have been wiser to abandon the guide books in favour of crayons and colouring books and a copy of 'Fairy Stories for Demented Children'. We spent the journey between Avallon and Lyon playing musical coach seats with three totally overtired and overwrought children. By the time we reached Avignon, the early morning sun rising over its famous bridge, we had come to the conclusion that several bottles of sleeping pills would have been far more useful than travel sickness pills. The only thing the children weren't was travel sick.

To be fair to the coach driver, there were ample rest stops during the journey south on the N1. To be fair to the children, I really do understand why they all need to answer the call of nature at the same time, three minutes after leaving the service area. With their usual immaculate sense of timing, the children finally succumbed to an advanced state of rigormortis just as we reached the entrance to the campsite.

Bedraggled as we may have appeared, at least the warm Mediterranean sunshine of Cavalaire sur Mer cheered us up considerably.

Our pre-erected tents, a double for the Model and I, and an adjacent one for the children, were a little basic, but the site was pleasantly set amongst pine trees, and had its own white-sanded beach. At the entrance to the campsite stood a wooden snack bar, offering warm beer, cold wine, cremated hamburgers, limp salad and *frites* with everything. The barman-cum-chef, we later found, also acted as an unqualified paramedic. Having unpacked and settled the children, we placed our allocated plastic table and chairs in front of the tents.

The next tent to our own was occupied by a couple in their late thirties, with two small sons.

"We're separated really," the wife explained, "but we thought we'd take this holiday together anyway."

"Yes, we're hoping –". We would never know what her husband hoped.

"Let's face it – "his wife interjected, "it couldn't get any worse!"

Given the confines of a camping holiday, this would prove to be an optimistic prediction.

Our nearest neighbours on the other side were a retired couple and 'professional campers'. It was only as we watched them unpack enough food to feed half the campsite, and setting up a stove, did we realise our oversight in this direction.

While others were unsuccessfully attempting to fit their baggage into one small tent, the professionals began to dig a neat, square hole in front of their tent. Into the hole they placed butter, milk and other perishables, replacing the turf lid – a refrigerated larder. As time went by, they were to prove their superior knowledge of all things under canvas, much to the chagrin of the rest of the campsite.

Following an orienteering trip around the camp, to find the laundrette and *bloc sanitaire,* we decided – the camp snack bar being closed – on an early night. Having settled the overtired children down, we attempted to find a comfortable position in our sleeping bags. Now I know why the French call them *un sac.*

On the verge of drifting into a much-needed sleep, we were awakened by the screams of the children. Grabbing the torch – one of the few useful things we had packed – I ran straight into the guy ropes of their tent. Amidst various curses, Anglo-Saxon and others, I threw open their tent flap to find them cowering in a corner in abject terror. Evidently, they had been attacked by (translation: seen) a man-eating toad with teeth the size of a dragon's. Trying hard not to laugh, I used the torch to search around the tent.

It was the first time I had seen toads with teeth. No, let's be more accurate: giant toads with fangs. I joined the children in the corner, much to my wife's disgust. I conceded it may have been a group hallucination brought on by exhaustion.

The next morning, we walked the two miles into the small port of Cavalaire sur Mer, with its quaint harbour of small boats and yachts; cafés and excellent quayside restaurants with numerous bars. Our first port of call was the local supermarket to stock up on basic necessities such as ham, cheese, bread, butter, sausage, fruit, beer and wine, not necessarily in that order. Due to a sleepless night on toad duty, we also needed torch batteries. It did not surprize me to find, in French, these are *des piles*. Very apt. It might easily apply to the result of overnight toad-spotting in wet grass...

Returning to the campsite, we set the table and chairs in the shade of a nearby pine for lunch al fresco. We had barely uncorked the *vin rouge* when attacked by kamikaze butterflies – at least I think they were butterflies. We decided unanimously to eat in town.

We settled on one of the many *Crepes Maison,* with their selection of chocolate, caramel, sugar and liqueur pancakes. We were nearly too late. It is worth remembering, that the cafés and restaurants usually close in the early afternoon for their siesta time.

Taking advantage of being in town, I sought out the office of the local *Syndicat d'Initiative* to present my *attestation* as a travel writer, and await the usual offers of assistance. Having scanned my credentials, with a shrug of her shoulder, she handed back my *attestation*.

"'Ave a nice 'oliday."

After the two-mile hike back to the campsite, we presumed the children would be tired. No, only the adults. We agreed they could go to the camp snack bar, and we would join them later. Mistake.

Upon settling the bill, it was obvious the children's French had improved in leaps and bounds, especially *un hamburger, un hot dog, glacé* and *limonade.* Just as I was about to leave the bar, the husband of the 'separated' holiday arrived. He sat down beside me on a bar stool.

"Hi! Your wife said you'd be here. Fancy a beer?"

Having sent the children back to the tents, and 'the Model' knowing my whereabouts, I accepted the invitation. It was only when he had finished his third beer while I sipped my first, that I began to realize where one of his marital problems might lie. As the afternoon surrendered to twilight, he refused to let me depart gladly – and he was built like a brick outhouse. I then had my worst suspicion confirmed – he had had his oesophagus removed and replaced with a plastic funnel.

By the time I returned to the tent – via a short respite in a ditch – 'the Model' and I were barely on speaking terms.

By the end of the first week, the pressure was beginning to tell. The campsite was deteriorating into a divorce centre, at least it was amongst we non-professional campers. Our retired, professional neighbours, so far as anyone could determine, had never had a cross word since their arrival. The whole campsite was beginning to hate them; they would go out of their way to avoid them as they sat outside their tent playing scrabble.

I had brought on holiday with me my pride and joy: my new, fully computerized 35mm camera. Point it and it would immediately adjust all settings for the perfect photo. Having loaded the camera in the shade, we set off for the mountaintop village of Gassin. The village is worth the hair-rising drive up the mountain; once there you are rewarded with an unsurpassed panorama over the gulf of St. Tropez. The village itself is a kaleidoscope of red-tiled houses and serpentine alleyways, clustered beneath the village church. The communal oven was still in use, providing the villagers' daily bread. It was only when I decided this was an ideal photo opportunity that the trouble started.

"Could you pass me the camera, please."

"I would if I had it."

"Pardon?"

"You had the camera darling, after you loaded the film, remember?"

"Yes, dearest, and I then handed it to you."

"No, oh blight of my life, I distinctly remember handing it to you."

"In that case, my lord and master, it's still where you left it."

Strange, how terms of endearment increase as a marriage deteriorates.

We passed the return journey in silence.

The camera having been found and handed in, the necessity of separate holidays was avoided. I, of course, apologised.

I hate apologising.

Especially when I'm in the wrong.

And when the children are listening.

We agreed to spend the next day on the beach. Once out of the campsite and across the main road, one was faced with an almost sheer drop to the beach below. To either side of this descent lay deep scrub, from which snakes meandered across the path. Who am I to dispute their right of way. Having finally reached the beach, I had to admit the sheltered cove was worth the climb back up. We purchased cold beer, lemonade and baguettes from the beach bar, and found a suitable spot to lay our towels. The cold beer did not stay cold for long in the Mediterranean sun, so I duly dug a hole in the sand in which to keep the beer cool, and went for a dip.

When I returned, I found the family had moved further down the beach, taking with them clothes, shoes and towels – all the evidence which might have provided a clue as to where the beer was buried.

The next day, we decided to spend the morning at the market and quayside of St. Tropez. At the market, I literally bumped into Brigitte Bardot with a basket full of vegetables. 'The Model' firmly steered me away from one of my teenage fantasies…

For the sun-seeker needing an all-over tan, St. Tropez's Tahiti Beach is the obvious choice. After walking for some fifty yards along the beach, we espied the couple who were about to prove my theory of 'The English Syndrome'.

We had met the retired banker and his wife a few days earlier while shopping in Grasse, the perfume centre of the South of France.

They were obviously enjoying their all-over tanning time until my fully-clothed entourage appeared.

"Hello again!"

Instant panic. My greeting had a similar effect as a husband and mistress being caught in bed by the wife. They sat up with a start, a flurry of hands and rapidly crossing legs. It is perfectly acceptable to bare all to strangers, particularly foreigners, but – horror of horrors – we were English and been introduced.

This is 'The English Syndrome'.

★ ★ ★ ★

The main pastime in St. Tropez is watching the 'beautiful people'. With the approach of the cocktail hour, St. Tropez comes into its own with the evening ritual of *Le Quai*. The promenading tourists look on with envy at the rich and famous holding pre-dinner cocktail parties on the stern decks of their yachts. The well-built 'minders' at the top of the gangway ensure no uninvited guests join the party. Mingling with the quayside onlookers are a smattering of the yacht-owners themselves, desperate to find out what their friends and rivals are wearing this season, what they are serving and – most importantly – to whom. The ultimate in 'keeping up with the Joneses'.

We opted for an al fresco dinner, and stumbled upon a *bouillabaisse* to kill for. This most French of Mediterranean cuisine is basically a fish casserole (as a Rolls Royce is just a car). Tomatoes, onions, leeks, cloves of garlic, cayenne pepper and olive oil provide the base.

To this is added firm-fleshed fish, soft-fleshed fish, eel, prawns, crayfish, potatoes and black pepper and sea salt to season, and an absolutely essential pinch of saffron. Served with garlic-rubbed croutons and a well-chilled dry white.

I stole the recipe.

So far, we seemed to have avoided the usual travails.

I should have known better than to tempt fate.

My downfall was the Ile Du Levant – an island famous for being given over entirely to naturism. It was the longest afternoon of my life.

Having taken the small ferry from Le Lavandou, we duly docked at the only jetty on the island. My first impression of the island was that of a rock rising out of the Mediterranean, surrounded by craggy cliffs and shingle coastline – ideal for the privacy demanded by the followers of nature.

After climbing what appeared to be a one-in - two hill to the summit of the island, the epicentre of its social life, we came to the small square with a bar/café and shop. The parasol-shaded tables of the café were crowded with naturists of varying hues – from the off-white of the newly-arrived to the deep, burnt sienna of the professionals. The majority wore a simple pouch in the interests of propriety and tourists.

After an excellent lunch of grilled crayfish, we were determined to spend the rest of the day gaining an all-over tan before the early evening return ferry. Despite our natural English reserve, 'the Model' and I had decided to bare all, presuming the children would follow our example.

Never presume anything.

Back at the jetty, we followed the signs along the rocky beach path until brought to an abrupt halt by a large red and white warning sign:

'No clothes beyond this point'.

From the sign, the beach was clearly visible, as were its naturists.

"Aargh! Mummy, look! Rudie Nudies!"

No amount of explaining, justifying, cajoling, bribing or threatening would persuade the girls to cast even a flip-flop. The remainder of the day, until the evening ferry, was spent climbing up and down the damned hill at an ever-decreasing pace. The doyen of child psychology who said that children adapt to new experiences more easily than adults, I would dearly like to meet.

That same evening back at the campsite, the unthinkable happened.

The 'professional campers' were preparing an evening meal on the primus stove in front of their tent. The husband was stirring the pan with a long-handled wooden spoon when his wife appeared behind him, glowering.

"You fool! You utter imbecile! You're stirring the soup the wrong way!"

As any half-wit knows, soup should always be stirred clockwise.

"My mother was right!"

With that, she attempted to slam the tent flap shut. Difficult.

From the stillness of deep-shadowed pines, a cheer went up around the campsite.

★ ★ ★ ★

Towards the end of this trip, we had the good fortune to meet a retired English gentleman of the old school. His appearance of a mad professor with a shock of white hair, belied his career as director of a well-known British medical institute. Now enjoying his retirement on the Côte D'Azur in his sister's villa, also enjoying her yacht. The villa had been designed by a cubist artist as a summer home, and was unique. The cubist influence was apparent from its many-tiered balconied façade. The roof garden offered him a particular joy: well-chilled white wine to the strains of Mozart and Verdi floating on the warm evening breeze.

In the well-stocked garden, the children never ceased to be impressed by the never-ending supply of freshly-squeezed orange juice, whilst the adults took advantage of the welcome shade of the orange grove to sip their pastis and water. This is an insidious drink.

It has a habit of creeping up on you, until you suddenly discover your legs don't work.

We decided to sober up with a bracing sail in the Med' on our host's sleek 24-foot yacht, to be joined by his visiting university student nephew and his friend.

In a gentle breeze, we set sail from Cavalaire Sur Mer to a secluded cove near La Lavandou. The children particularly enjoyed taking turns at the helm – this was just as well, as the adults were in no condition.

Dropping anchor in the cove, the nephew and friend decided to snorkel. Our attention was attracted to his shouting off the port bow.

"My mask doesn't work – I can't see out of it!"

"Spit in it!" we shouted in unison.

Looking somewhat puzzled, he turned to his right and spat into the Mediterranean. Replacing his still-clouded mask, he gave the thumbs up and disappeared beneath the surface.

"At best a 2.2," his uncle said with some sadness, referring to the 'drinker's degree'.

Back in the villa gardens, during the course of a dinner of avocado, prawns and freshly caught lobster, the children were allowed to dine *à la Francais*. This involved them drinking wine and water. Gradually, the ratio of wine to water is increased until, in theory, their palate can differentiate between the wines and their quality.

Deep in conversation, we adults paid little interest in the children's progress.

Mistake.

Unbeknownst to us, two of them, having decided they did not appreciate the wine and water, had been exchanging their glasses for their sister's empty one. She certainly appreciated it.

Suddenly, the wine-loving seven-year-old leapt onto the long table and ran its length towards her mother. She did not stop. She launched herself off the table like a missile, screaming hysterically "Mummy! I love you! I'll never leave you!"

Landing on 'the Model's' lap, they both toppled backwards onto the garden, still attached to the chair.

"My God!" 'the Model' managed to gasp, "she's hysterical!"

"No," stated our host and myself in unison, "she's drunk."

She slept for most of the journey home.

Chapter Three
The Mayflower Mystery

My travails began somewhat earlier than I expected, when I flew to New York.

My baggage flew to Hong Kong.

I was left with only the clothes I stood up in. The airline said this was no problem. The airline did not have to wear the same suit for the foreseeable future. They explained they paid compensation for lost baggage. It was the first, and last time I ever tried to buy a whole wardrobe for £60. This ran out after buying one shirt, one pair of trousers and an extremely cheap blazer (the sleeves of which fell off a week later).

My baggage reappeared four weeks later. I am not impressed by airline compensation.

There is something more than a little scary about getting behind the wheel of a rental car, and driving straight into six lanes of the freeway in rush hour at JFK Airport, and, amidst blaring horns, flashing headlamps and shouted expletives, finding oneself in midtown Manhattan.

At least the North American habit of adhering to a grid system of streets and avenues, made navigation (pre-SatNav) easier than on other Continents. However, when driving an unfamiliar rental car, turning on the windscreen wipers when meaning to indicate, there is no guarantee that, once familiar with the traffic signs and laws, it is safe to drive. Driving on the right is not a problem. The dimensions of several American cars – slightly smaller than a truck - is.

I would advise anyone contemplating renting a car to take out the optional Collision Damage Waiver (CDW). It is also advisable to stick to the larger, well-known rental car companies. A sub-compact car is usually a better choice as there is less of it to damage. Only once did I ignore my own advice, which nearly proved fatal.

In Toronto, I rented a car from a company called 'Rent-A-Wreck'. It could not be faulted under the Trade Descriptions Act. The daily rental charge was less than a couple of cold beers, hence the attraction. Thus, I found myself driving in a blizzard down the Queen Elizabeth Way when the brakes failed. After spinning around several times, the car came to a halt across two lanes, broadside on to oncoming traffic. I closed my eyes. Unable to see me in time through the blizzard, cars were spinning in every direction attempting to avoid me. One didn't bother. A large, blue coupe, or, more specifically, its radiator, joined me in the front of the car. On impact, it managed to dislodge most of my car's excessive rust – which accounted for most of its chassis.

As roughly the same traffic laws apply in Canada as England, the blue car driver and I agreed to take the next exit from the freeway and exchange details while waiting for the Highway Patrol. Keeping my car facing in the right direction was a feat in itself. As we reached the exit slip road, the blue car driver could only watch as I continued ever onward. The steering would not turn right.

Reaching the city, it took me two hours to reach the rental car lot due to the car's steering only turning left. The rental company were very understanding: they agreed to refund me all rental charges in exchange for me dropping charges of attempted homicide.

Returning (a new) rental car to Toronto Airport, I parked where directed by a member of staff. Back in England, I received a summons to appear at Toronto District Court for non-payment of a parking fine. This was not surprizing, as I had never received one. Evidently, I had been directed to the wrong parking bay. I explained on the telephone that the cost of a six-thousand-mile round-trip to defend a C$30 fine had little to commend it, unless they would care to pay for my extradition. They declined.

The pre-photocard English Driving Licence was a godsend – at least it was to me, especially if turned inside out in its plastic wallet.

"Okay," drawled the motorcycle cop as he removed his gloves and dark glasses, "you in a race, Mac?"

I handed over my driving licence as requested.

"What the hell is this, buddy – a joke?"

I looked suitably confused.

"That's what you asked for officer, my driving licence."

"Your driver's licence? Where the hell's the rest of it?"

"There is no rest of it," I explained patiently, "and no photo – all the details are there, encoded by the DVLC in Swansea."

I smiled. He didn't.

"Who the hell are the DVLC? You a spy or somethin'?"

Totally defeated in trying to make sense of the licence, he threw it into the car with ill-concealed frustration.

"Okay, Mac. Get outta here – and watch your ass!"

I did as he suggested.

★ ★ ★ ★

I was not usually nervous in small aircraft, until I found myself as the only passenger in a single-engine Piper at Welland Aero Club in

Ontario, close to the US border, heading out over the lake towards Niagara Falls Airport. At the controls, a Transatlantic 747 pilot and friend. I was not aware that in his free time he was also a 'barnstormer', an acrobatics pilot, as was about to be proved in spectacular fashion.

As we approached the Horseshoe Falls, he called the tower for landing clearance, as we overflew the thunderous cascade of water.

Suddenly, he turned to me and asked:

"You want a closer look?"

I was never one to miss an opportunity.

Circling the Falls once more, he called the tower and reported engine trouble, requesting permission to lose height and 'throttle out'. He suddenly banked the plane and side-slipped towards the rocks below. I was thinking I should have worn my brown trousers.

The noise from the Falls drowned out the sound of the engine, as he flew straight for the terrifying wall of water that is Niagara Falls.

At the last possible moment, he pulled out and, at full throttle, seemed to climb straight up the Falls. Levelling out, he circled the crowd of cheering, waving sightseers below.

It had proven to be a once in a lifetime experience.

Once is enough.

★ ★ ★ ★

There is more to New York than shopping: watch the ever-changing shadows in the skyscraper canyons from the 86th floor observation deck of the Empire State building or visit 'the village', the Bowery and Skid Row. From Times Square and Broadway, head for Little Italy and Chinatown or take a ferry to Liberty and Ellis Island, now an Immigration Museum, illustrating the USA's reputation as 'the melting pot of nations'.

It would be a little much to expect Central Park's 840 acres to be crime-free. Less publicized are its two zoos, skating rink, tennis courts, riding trails and mile upon mile of jogging paths.

By night, the City gains its second breath, with its theatres, cabaret shows, nightclubs, themed bars and multi-ethnic restaurants. It is not difficult to party until the sun rises over the East River – not, of course, that I would dream of doing so on expenses. One of the more civilised ways to see the panoramic lights of New York is over dinner at The Rainbow Room on the 64th floor of the RCA Building.

Apart from the street vendors' hot dogs, a must-have, food can present a problem in translation: chips become crisps, and fries become chips. A steak remains a steak, and Americans take their steak very seriously. A medium steak is likely to be rare, a rare steak almost raw, and a well-done will be medium. Their mantra is 'undercooked rather than cremated'. I totally agree. In the south-west, I have heard a waiter asked for a well-done steak, suggest to the diner he eat elsewhere. If English, play it safe and order a medium-well. A speciality is a New York Smothered (with fried onions) Steak.

Rarely, I have been known to visit an 'adult club' in various countries. New York was no exception. I was leaving the club on Lexington

Avenue around three in the morning, when a shapely brunette stepped out of the shadows.

"Hi sugar. Looking for company?"

Her hands were everywhere – and I mean everywhere.

I explained that, in my present condition, it would be a waste of her time and my money. She disappeared even more quickly than she had appeared. So did my wallet.

In the lobby of my hotel, one of New York's finest was leaning against the reception desk. I reported my mugging. I wondered why he wasn't making notes.

"Well," he advised laconically, "I guess you could go down the precinct station and fill in a report, but, to be honest, fella, you're the seventeenth tonight."

I decided not to bother.

Back in my hotel room, I took a shower before bed. Still naked, I walked over to the window, with its view over the Chrysler Building and Manhattan's skyline. Suddenly, there was a blue flash of static electricity from the metal radiator under the window. Unfortunately, the mini lightning bolt connected with my genitals.

There are many ways to end an evening in Manhattan, but I would not recommend self-emasculation as one of them.

One New York attraction the majority of visitors never see, is its railroad terminus, Grand Central Station. The 42nd Street entrance leads to a huge mausoleum of pseudo-classical architecture, teeming with commuters, and home to fast food stalls and cafes and shops ranging from fashion to key-cutting. It is simply unique, with an atmosphere all its own.

★ ★ ★ ★

Boston is less of a culture shock for the English. Founded in 1630 and named after Boston in Lincolnshire, it has a deep sense of its historical importance. Its gold-domed State House is known as 'The Cradle of Liberty', and the North Street Church contains the oldest clock in a public building (1723), and the first metal pipe organ in the Colonies from 1775. It was from the church's tower that Paul Revere swung his lantern to warn of the coming of the British. The Revere House, dating from 1680, is the only remaining house from that period. The memorial to the Battle of Bunker Hill can hardly be missed – the 221-foot granite obelisk is remarkably similar to that of Cleopatra's Needle on London's Embankment.

The harbour is home to the USS Constitution – 'Old Ironsides' – the oldest commissioned frigate still operating in the US Navy. Unfortunately, it was used by the British against its builders in the War of 1812, when the British reduced the then White House to ashes. When in Boston, I have found it better not to mention this.

One of the pitfalls of being in Boston is simply being English. I blame 'The Daughters of the Revolution'. Sat in the lobby of my hotel, I was talking to a young lady when her mother came bearing down upon us like a ship in full sail. Her look left no doubt that she was convinced I was trying to seduce her daughter. Once I had the opportunity to speak, this brought about a complete change in attitude.

"Oh, I'm so sorry. I didn't realize you were English. Oh, I just *love* your accent!" I pointed out that I was not the one with an accent.

"Our family came over on the 'Mayflower'," she stated proudly, sizing me up as potential marriageable material. 'We're blue blooded – do you have a title?"

Over several years, I have calculated, based on introductions to the Pilgrims' descendants, that the 'Mayflower' was only slightly larger than the latest cruise liner. This called for immediate action: I called my friend in Plymouth.

Some days later, I was pinned against a wall by yet another descendant of a 'Mayflower' pilgrim. I reached into my breast pocket and produced a little black book.

"I'm sorry – what was your name again? I'll check it for you against the passenger manifest."

The word quickly spread that I had the passenger list.

End of problem.

★ ★ ★

Extracts from my travel notes: 1975

Saturday:

Arrived Majorca/Mallorca. Base this trip: the capital, Parma.

Check in. Credentials to Tourist Office. Dinner in hotel.

Sunday:

Planning day. Brief: recommend resorts suitable for a quiet and relaxing holiday for the older visitor, the opposite of Palma Nova and Magaluf in the south, christened 'Blackpool in the Sun'.

Monday:

1½ hour drive north-west to the Pollensa and Cala san Vincente area, sheltered by Tramuntana mountains. Hotels built before 1960s concrete onslaught. Hotels on Pollensa Promenade retain the genteel air of the 1920s. If looking to party – forget it.

Tuesday:

40 miles east of Palma to Porto Cristo and San Severa. Porto Cristo low key and quiet, but seems to have a foot in both camps. Attraction: Caves of Drach.

Wednesday:

As per demographic target of ABC1 middle aged couples, will be recommending the more relaxing north-west and east coasts resorts as a panacea for Magaluf/Palma Nova. Parma remains a 'must visit' for the Cathedral and Basilica de Sant. Francesc.

Thursday:

Shortlist recommended restaurants: the Ca'n Manlol and the terrace by the sea of the Ola del Mar in Palma; Il Giardino in the square in Pollensa; the terrace of the Roland Restaurant in Porto Cristo.

Friday:

AM: Arrange flight back to UK for tomorrow.

PM: No flight for tomorrow. Editor can't get me on a (freebee) flight until Wednesday. Advantage: "Whatever you need, just sign for it at the hotel, and put receipts in for anything else when you get back".

I love unlimited expenses.

Tuesday:

Shouldn't have gone to the disco last night – pulled a muscle in my back. Painful. Lie on balcony rest of day in the sun – heat therapy.

Woken up by sun going down. Couldn't move. Finally made it to bathroom like an arthritic tortoise. Wish I hadn't looked in mirror. Bright scarlet face and torso covered in mosquito bites, one on right eyelid swollen to four times its normal size. In too much pain to sleep.

I wish I was home.

Wednesday:

'The Model' and children are meeting me in Arrivals. I loped across the concourse in a low crouch (pulled muscle worse), glowing incandescent red, right eye totally closed, and a stuffed donkey under one arm.

Waiting families and friends scattered in horror. I must have looked like a hybrid of a badly-mauled lobster thermidor and Charles Laughton as *'The Hunchback of Notre Dame'* on a bad day, a donkey under one arm and pursued by two policemen attracted by the panic.

It took almost thirty minutes to prise the children from their mother's legs.

We almost left the motorway via the central reservation, as all hell broke loose in the back of the car.

"Daddy, it's the donkey – its alive!" they screamed in unison.

Onto hard shoulder. Investigate. Donkey *was* breathing. Polythene wrapping appeared to be inhaling and exhaling.

Tonight, children had nightmares.

So did I.

Thursday:

Killed donkey and burned evidence. 'Manũel' the burro, had been stuffed with several kilos of nails. It was, in fact, a cunningly disguised Spanish anti-personnel mine.

Addendum:

Even now, occasionally in my nightmares, I am running through a cavernous shopping mall pursued by a three-legged donkey, a police armed response unit and a dozen bright-red hunchbacks.

Chapter Four
Sunstroke and Sanitary Towels

For a feature on family holidays in the Greek Islands, I decided to avoid the more obvious southerly destinations and chose the scattered islands of the Sporades in the north-west Aegean, to the west of the Pelion Peninsular of mainland Greece.

Skiathos, or 'Host of Shadows', is the westernmost island, named by its first inhabitants, the Karians, due to the dense woods of pine trees. With over 66 beaches, Skiathos has more than any other Aegean island.

Skiathos port has been used as a safe haven through the centuries, from the Athenians, Romans and Byzantines to the Venetians and Greece during its War of Independence in 1821. It was also the base of the British Mediterranean Fleet during the Second World War. The present town of Skiathos was founded in 1829, when the populace abandoned the fortress town of Kastro, officially becoming a town in 1965.

The only surfaced road on the island was the 7-mile coastal drive from the town to koukounaries; all the other roads were really dirt tracks 'unsuitable for motor vehicles'.

That, we were to find, was an understatement.

Prior to the arrival of the airport runway and tourists, the only 'roads' on the island were mule tracks for access to the olive groves.

Skiathos Town – or Chora – is the island's centre for shopping, dining al fresco and nightlife. At the harbourside bars, cafés and tavernas, people-watching and yacht-spotting are as popular as in St. Tropez. As one of the most sophisticated of the Aegean islands, Skiathos is popular with private yachts, flying the flags of many nations. Lying on koukounaries beach, we watched a yacht the size of a cruise liner drop anchor offshore. It had a helipad and a full-size swimming pool which extended and retracted into the side of the yacht. It was only later we were told the yacht's owner was Michael

Jackson, with Diana Ross aboard as his guest on this cruise.

On all Greek islands it is difficult to escape the bouzouki, similar to a balalaika crossed with a lute. I blame 'Zorba the Greek'. In fact, the bouzouki originated in the Orient, and was brought to Greece as recently as 1922. At one time, it was banned by the government as representing the resistance, and was forced underground; now it has become synonymous with Greece.

Mandraki beach, noted for its reddish cliffs, has no shade. Teenaged second son has no sense. For several years I tried to find any sign of an IQ, without success. Despite my advice to start tanning slowly and increase the time in the sun each day, they decided that a first day of eight hours tanning time was a good idea.

Second son suffered the worst. His forehead swelled to three times its normal size, resulting in an impersonation of a Neolithic man, without his club. We had no choice but to keep him indoors to stop him terrifying small children. His elder sibling, the medical student, diagnosed water on the brain due to ample cavity space.

"Very helpful – not!" said mother ('the Nurse' – next wife).

For the next three days, Neolithic man smothered his entire body with aftersun, aloe vera and anything else he could find (we hid the breakfast yoghurt).

Krassa is the beach for an all-over tan, having been one of the first designated nudist beaches. There is a choice of Big Banana, popular for topless sunbathing, or Little Banana, around the point and more secluded, where no restrictions apply. 'The Nurse' commented I must have been pleased to find the adjectives Big and Little applied only to the beaches. Uncalled for.

The eldest teenage son felt it necessary to state he was not at all interested in the topless females around him. He was on page 37 of his novel. After lunch on the beach and 'tanned out' after several hours, we prepared to leave the beach. Eldest was on page 38.

We took a leisurely boat trip to the comparatively peaceful island of Skopelos. It is not usually on the atheist's list of things to do, having a dozen monasteries and convents and over 360 chapels. Skopelos is one of the less crowded islands, offering sandy beaches and opportunities to swim, snorkel, cycle and horseride. The island gets its name from the reef and rocky outcrops along its coastline. The town's steep, narrow alleyways of whitewashed houses are ablaze with the colours of their carefully tended window boxes and pots. The island's ancient plane trees lend a relaxed atmosphere to the waterfront shops and tavernas; overlooking the town is the imposing Venetian Castle, at the other end of town is the monastery of Episkopi. From the island's summit, reached by a stairway from the quayside, panoramic views look over the church, port and turquoise-blue Aegean Sea.

We thought this would be the ideal opportunity to teach youngest how to snorkel.

Wrong.

Following CPR on the beach due to her sucking the Aegean down the breathing tube instead of exhaling, we persevered. After some ten minutes, she ran from the sea, screaming.

"Help! I saw a fish – it's after me!"

No amount of persuasion could convince her that was the whole point of snorkelling. We gave up.

Back in Koukounaries, I visited the local shop. But, only once. At the cash desk, the girl started sniffing and leaning in my direction.

"Oh! I love your husband's smell!"

This, unfortunately, to my wife.

"Ambre Solaire," 'the Nurse' stepped in.

Outside the shop, I tried to explain to her that in times past, before perfume, aftershave and deodorant, individual body smell had been imperative in attracting a potential mate. This made absolutely no difference. Unjustly, I was banned from going within 500 yards of the shop for the duration of the trip.

In the interests of the eldest's further education, it had been decided by 'the Nurse' that I would take him to the Oracle at Delphi, despite the fact it was at the other side of the Greek mainland. The Blue Dolphin hydrofoil took us to Aghios Konstandinos to pick up a coach across Greece, returning the same day – a twelve-hour journey, through Atalandi, Melessina, Schimatara, Malakass, bypassing Athens and continueing past Elefsina and Magara towards the plains of Amfissa. Even before the tortuous drive into the mountains, I had lost the will to live.

Finally, overlooking the Gulf of Corinth, we reached Mount Parnassus, home of the Delphic Oracle. For the ancient Greeks, Delphi was the navel of the Earth, where two eagles released by Zeus, had flown from opposite ends of the world and met on this spot. The young god Apollo, 'the brightest and best of all the gods', patron of music and the arts, had slain the dragon Python here. At this place, sacred to Gaia the Earth goddess and her daughters, Apollo founded the Oracle in a cleft in the rock-face. It was to become the moral and religious capital of the classical world for centuries to come.

In reality, Delphi's power was based on its prodigious wealth. City and Island States stretching from Syracuse in Sicily to Lydia in Asia Minor, vied with each other to offer the Oracle the richest gifts. Wars were fought at the Oracle's behest, and no important decisions of

State were taken between 600 and 500BC without its advice.

In 191BC, control of the Oracle passed to the Romans, and Delphi obeyed the orders of the Emperor in Rome. In Emperor Hadrian's reign, despite his support, Delphi was losing its followers to Christianity. Emperor Julian (360 to 362AD) attempted to revive the ancient religion, but without success. The cult of Apollo was ended.

To climb Mount Parnassus to the Oracle and to the Stadium of the Pythian Games at 7,000 feet, takes stamina and a good pair of boots. The first steps of the climb are the Sacred Way, the ruins of the Roman agora; the facades of the Roman-built shops can be clearly seen.

At the Sanctuary of Athena, on the right is the Stoa of the Athenians with its polygonal walls, its Doric columns dating from 500BC. The Treasury of the Athenians was erected from 490 to 489BC with 10% of its spoils from the Battle of Marathon. To the right is the Stone of the Sybil, where Herophile, the first Sybil, delivered her oracles, including her prediction of the Trojan War.

The Temple of Apollo dates from the 4th Century BC. The ancient Greeks believed the first temple had been made of laurel, the second of beeswax and wings, the third of bronze and the fourth of porous stone, destroyed by fire in 584BC. In 510BC it was rebuilt, but an earthquake in 373BC reduced it to rubble, but it was rebuilt by 330BC. Few people were admitted to the inner temple, containing a gold statue of Apollo.

In the Oracle itself, the will of Apollo was made known by the Pythia – in its early years a young virgin, later a venerated woman over fifty years of age – who lived her life in the temple. First, the applicant cleansed himself in the water of the Castilian Spring, paid a fee and sacrificed a young goat on the altar of Apollo, but the animal must have no defects. As a sign the god was at home and the day convenient, water was poured over the goat. If it trembled, then the day was propitious. There were obviously few days when it was not.

The Pythia, having been cleansed with spring water, and her attendant priests, would then burn barley and flour in the immortal hearth. She then descended to the adyton beneath the nave, and drank water from the Cassostis Spring of the shrine. Once the applicant asked his question, the Pythia, chewing laurel leaves, mounted the sacred tripod and touched the carved navel while inhaling the 'spirit' emanating from the rock and fell into a trance.

It is now believed 'the spirit' was hallucinogenic, and the Pythia stoned. As she spoke, in verse or prose, her attendants would interpret her words. A typically ambiguous piece of advice from the Oracle, was that given to Croesus, King of Lydia, whose gifts to the Oracle included a solid gold lion weighing 600 pounds. This advice was that, if he should wage war on the Persians, he would destroy a great power. He duly went to war, was defeated, and the great power destroyed was his own. From the Pythia's point of view: 'Result!'.

Beyond the Oracle lies the 2nd Century BC theatre. Higher still is the Stadium of the Pythian Games. On this visit, I never made it past the Temple of Apollo.

The previous day, I had been the target of every mosquito living in the swamp of the Nature Reserve behind the beach. Badly bitten on both ankles, 'the Nurse' pronounced her professional diagnosis:

"Of course, they're not infected!"

The next morning, she looked again.

"Oh, my God! They're infected!"

Being due to leave for Delphi, we were somewhat pushed for time. The infected bites were lanced with a hot needle, and antiseptic cream and dressings applied. Unfortunately, we had no dressings. The only things we could find as a substitute were sanitary towels. That is how I came to be painfully climbing Mount Parnassus with my feet bound in sanitary towels.

I had surreptitiously tagged on the end of a group of American tourists being led by an English-speaking guide. By the time we attempted to climb up to the theatre, the pain in my feet was horrendous. The tour guide was becoming more and more impatient with the straggler.

"Will you *please* keep up with the group."

"I *can't!*" I screamed. "My sanitary towels are slipping – you fool!"

The group of Americans stood in stunned silence.

★ ★ ★ ★

I have always said you are safer in a 4WD.

As usual, I was wrong.

After several abortive attempts in the open-topped 4WD jeep to find a dirt-track road which did not lead us back into Skiathos Town, we threw in the towel and headed for the mountains of the north coast, to search for the ancient capital of Kastro.

Driving beyond Aselinos, the cliff-edge (and I mean edge) track, betwixt the clifftop and the sea, had become so badly eroded it became necessary to avoid the seaward edge of the track – and the rocks below – by hugging the cliff wall on our right, the jeep tilting dangerously.

Then we came to a stretch with no track at all – it had fallen into the sea far below. As trying to reverse would have been tantamount to suicide, the only option was to edge forward as slowly as possible with the right-hand side wheels gripping the cliff-side with the jeep at maximum pre-roll tilt. I refused the offsprings' pleading to leave the jeep, instead ordering them to lean to their right, as far over as possible, adding weight to the two wheels which were on firm ground. At a 45° angle, we inched forward until back on the track. 'The Nurse' kissed me in gratitude for saving their lives, then slapped me for putting them in danger in the first place…

Eventually, shaken and stirred, we came to the secluded beach of Kehria and took the track downward – we'd worry about the upward later – and the beach taverna: two tables, only open in the summer. Over a plate of squid, the owner explained he, as did his usual customers, came by boat. How sensible.

Finally, we reached the northernmost headland of the island and the old capital of Kastro. Here, even the dirt-track road petered out, the only access being on foot. Perched on a rocky outcrop, the 14th Century fortress had been a defence against marauding pirates and home to the island's entire population, not beginning to be abandoned until 1829. Two small churches remain standing as well as a half-destroyed mosque and two of the water storage tanks used to pour scalding water down onto the enemy. Nothing now remains of the fortress's tower and the Venetian Governor's Residence.

Ignoring our map, presumably drawn by a blind cartographer, we eventually joined the coastal road, more by accident by design.

Our 'farewell dinner' at Willi's Taverna was an unmitigated disaster. On the way to the tavern, the eldest put his sister in a headlock. Had she jerked her head, her neck would have broken. She could not breathe and was turning blue. He refused his mother's order to release the lock. In reflex mode, I launched a high sidekick to his throat (as you do) as a rapid and effective solution. Unfortunately, his mother leapt in front of him in his defence. I was forced to change the direction of the kick in mid-air to avoid decapitating his mother, and connected with thin air, accompanied by the 'twang' of a snapped hamstring.

The pain was indescribable. I could not stand, let alone walk. I was not prepared to ruin our last evening and, half carried, I made it in to Willi's by crawling up the disabled ramp on all fours. Everyone went for the *kleftika* for dinner; I went for a dozen heavy duty painkillers, a bottle of Ouzo and an icepack strapped to my hamstring.

With no taxi available, 'the Nurse', with the painkillers, tried to organise the boys into a pair of human crutches. Next problem: the eldest needed to get into Skiathos Town as he'd arranged to meet 'some guys' at a nightclub. To add insult to injury, he 'borrowed' the money for entrance fee, drinks and a cab. His mother was not impressed.

I returned to the UK in a wheelchair.

★ ★ ★ ★

Santorini in the Cyclades islands. According to Plato: 'The Ancient Kingdom of Atlantis'. In 1500BC, the volcanic eruption of the island – then Thera – was one of the largest the world had ever known, and created a tsunami which destroyed the Minoan civilization of Crete, some seventy miles to the south.

In a rental car, we travelled to Mount Elias, at 1,829 feet the highest peak of the Perissa Mountains, for a photo shoot of the panoramic views over the coast. Every frustrated archaeologist should head for the Minoan excavations at Akrotiri. It is an uphill climb, but the mobility-challenged can usually make it as pillion passenger on the back of one of the local

- 68 -

youths' motorbikes, as did I. The prehistoric settlement in the south of the island, dates from the late Bronze Age (1650 – 1500BC). The finds proved the site was continually inhabited from the middle of the Fifth Millennium BC. The ruins are well-preserved and provide an accurate picture of Aegean society. Its wall frescoes are the earliest known examples of large-scale wall paintings in Europe.

For lunch, we stopped at the Viychada Taverna in the hills. At that time, my mobility was assisted by a reproduction gold-topped Edwardian cane. Following an excellent lunch, complemented by a local wine made from the Assyrtiko grape, the owner approached me and pointed to my cane.

"I like your cane. You give me cane, and no bill for lunch. Fair – yes?"

As the cane had cost me only £10 in England and our bill came to over £40, I thought this was very fair. The Greek Immigration Officers on every island I subsequently visited, are still trying to work out why I am travelling with a dozen gold-topped Edwardian walking canes.

★ ★ ★ ★

Kos, the third-largest island of the Dodecanese. Its population of only a little over 30,000 is substantially increased by the number of holidaymakers in the summer season. We flew into Hippocrates International Airport, some 13 miles south-west of Kos Town, the island's capital. With good reason, I associate the Dodecanese being an integral contributor to my travails abroad.

Taking a cab from the airport, we settled in to our hotel in Kefalos Bay, next to the Aegean Sea. Had it been any closer, it would have been in the Aegean Sea. Following a beachside lunch, 'the Nurse' purchased an electric jug kettle at the small shop over the road. This was a necessity – without her morning ritual of a cup of unpacked Earl Grey, she is fit company for neither man nor beast. Unfortunately, the kettle did not have an automatic breaker.

We had settled on our balcony with a glass of wine, when we were engulfed by acrid black smoke coming out of the room via the sliding door. The now empty kettle had reached its ignition temperature, and had melted into liquid plastic. The flames proceeded to set fire to the curtains.

I did what I do best. I shouted instructions to 'the Nurse'.

"Unplug it, throw it out onto the balcony and put it out!"

In pure panic, she unplugged what was left of the kettle and swung it by its flex out onto the balcony. Returning with our breakfast mango juice, she poured it over the kettle and curtains. Unfortunately, part of the melted metal thermostat had dripped into the runner of the balcony's sliding door, welding it open. Being too cowardly to report it to the management, we were unable to close it for the rest of our stay. This meant, by necessity, we were forced to purchase several electrically operated mosquito repellents.

A short walk up the beach lie the remains of the pillars of the Basilica of Agios Stephanos, built in the 6th century AD on the shores of the Aegean Sea. Opposite the temple, some quarter mile out into the Aegean, is the small, uninhabited island of Kastri, with its blue-roofed, whitewashed church. In times past, a rope stretched across to the island to aid visitors. Now, the only way to reach the island is to swim or by small boat. The tradition remains that, having reached the island, the church bell must be rung to announce the visitor's arrival.

This visit happened to coincide with 'the Nurse's birthday, which we had decided to celebrate at the hotel's beachside restaurant. Before ordering a dozen fresh oysters, I checked on the price of champagne.

"Is 16 Euros a bottle,' the waitress smiled.

I smiled back. In England, I usually paid £28 per bottle – this was £12.

"Are you sure?"

"Ochee – is 16 Euroes."

I ordered two, which duly arrived in their ice buckets, one opened and the other in waiting.

Following excellent red snapper and swordfish, I signalled for the bill. The champagne was billed at €60 a bottle, a total of €120 – or £90. I pointed this out to the waitress.

"Ochee – is 16 Euros – yes?"

"No," I pointed to the bill and stated in Greek, "that is 60 – not 16!"

"Sorry – my English she is not so good."

Before we left, we bought her a Greek-English Phrase Book. How were we to know she was Slovakian?

The next morning, I showered, shaved and brushed my teeth. Then I took a mouthful of mint green mouthwash. It was not mouthwash. It was the green shampoo. In shock, I swallowed it. Not the best way to start a day.

To Kos Town to catch yet another ferry, but first, lunch by the agora, the ancient marketplace. A few yards up from the Agora stands Hippocrates' plane tree, a national monument surrounded by scaffolding to save it from toppling onto the tourists, and where, history would have us believe, he lectured his students. Not a bad trick, given the plane tree itself proved to have been planted after his death.

Catching the ferry for the island of Symi, darkness had fallen by the time we arrived and took the obligatory canary yellow Mercedes taxi to our hotel overlooking Nimborio Bay. Or we thought we had.

"*Sirnomi* -I go no more. No taxi no more. You get out *now, neh?*"

"*Viakis!*" I threw my arms open in gesture, but the taxi driver was already unloading our luggage onto the side of the road.

"Is no road," he pointed ahead of us.

He was right. The surfaced road came to a sudden end, replaced by a series of deep potholes sown into the road in a random pattern. I could see his point.

Staggering under our baggage, we began to hike the three miles to the Bay. The gods smiled upon us. After fifty yards, we bumped, literally, in the dark, into an old lady by her house on the hillside. She phoned our hotel to come and pick us up. I understand the road has now been improved. That wouldn't have been difficult.

Symi is rightly considered to be the most beautiful of all the islands of Greece. Only six miles long and five miles wide, with a population of only 2,500, its 'capital', Symi Town, is divided by its harbour into north and south, spanned by a stone bridge. Approaching by sea, Gialos, the small harbour of Symi, lined with tavernas, bars and shops, gives the initial impression of a Classical Greek town. The island had the foresight to ban the building of the more typically concrete, whitewashed, blue-roofed houses, allowing only the neo-classical architectural style. Consequently, the harbour was surrounded by the spectrum of magnificent pillared houses in pastel shades of pink, green, lemon, yellow, red – every colour but white. The effect is breathtaking. Little wonder it is listed as an historical scheduled monument.

Looking down over Gialos like a rich relative, is the larger, residential Chorio, aloof from the visiting tourists with access by 500 stairs from the harbourside, or by the only decent road on the island, two miles of asphalt, paid for by its residents.

Next stop: a short visit by ferry from Kardamena on Kos to the volcano of Nisyros, population 938. The volcano is its claim to fame, classified, rather like myself, as 'active sleeping'. Its age is estimated to be 4,000 years, and renowned as one of the world's best-preserved hypothermal craters. Nisyros' narrow alleyways and lanes create a maze interspersed with small squares of intricately - patterned black and white mosaics. This trip I avoided the waiting travail by boarding the last ferry sixteen minutes early. It sailed fifteen minutes early. One to me.

Recently, I was asked to update my feature on Kos, this time concentrating on the historical. Having revisited the ancient agora and the 11th Century castle of the Knight Templars – The Order of Saint John of Jerusalem – overlooking the harbour, I centred my piece on Hippocrates' terraced Asklepieion, his medical school cum hospital. Unfortunately, I decided to become a tourist and took the Kos City Train Bus. I should have known better.

The red-painted 'train', modelled on a 19th Century US engine, complete with cowcatcher, towed several open, roofed wooden carriages offered a circular tour by what were laughingly called 'roads'. As usual, I chose the worst possible seat – over the wheel. As we progressed, the train seemed determined to find every pothole on the island. With every lurch, I was literally thrown into the air, landing heavily back on my hardwood seat. This may, perhaps, have been just bearable had I not been travelling with two compacted vertabrae, a crushed disc and a broken rib and clavicle at the time. The things I do for England.

(I have no intention, in this book, of divulging how I came by my injuries).

I can only assume my fellow passengers put my screams down to panic at travelling over five miles per hour. I have never been so relieved to reach my destination.

Hippocrates – the Father of Medicine – had been born at Kefalos on Kos in 460BC. The Asklepieion, the medical school he founded, would last for a thousand years. Centuries ahead of his time, Hippocrates declared illnesses were not sent by the gods, but linked to the living conditions and lifestyle of the patient, also giving them nutritional advice. He was against suicide and abortion, but believed in patient confidentiality. Hippocrates' 'Asklipiad' of the 5th Century BC forms the origins of today's Hippocratic Oath.

The first terrace of the Asklepieion contained rooms for visitors and families, examinations and recuperation; the second terrace was used for hydrotherapy, and contained temples to Apollo and Asklepios. The third terrace had rooms for the sick, with its own temples, where a staircase linked the terrace to the Sacred Groves, where it was forbidden to give birth or die.

Thanks to my ride on the red train, severe pain precluded me from climbing the terraces. I cheated. I rewrote my notes from a previous visit. It is impossible to plagiarise one's own work.

By Kos harbour on my last day, I witnessed a scene I found somewhat disturbing. A crocodile of men, women and children of various ages were being escorted by blue uniforms along the quayside. It was only later I discovered that what I had witnessed was the arrival of some of the first illegal immigrants from the Turkish Coast, four miles away.

Chapter Five
'This One's Broken.'

1755 was a very good year not to be in the westernmost capital of mainland Europe. The Great Earthquake of that year destroyed 85% of the city of Lisbon, killing over 30,000 people. The event shocked the whole of Europe. However, it did lead to the decision to demolish what remained of the city and rebuild it as the modern metropolis of its time, reflected in its broad boulevards, parks, monuments and Opera House.

When the Romans ruled the city from 250BC, it had already been in existence for over a millennium. By the 5th Century, the Germanic tribes had taken the city. The Moors ruled in the 8th Century, and were still in control when Portugal was reconquered by Christianity, the city becoming the nation's capital in 1255.

The most impressive way of entering the city is by sea, sailing past the Tower of Balem and under the ten-mile long Vasco da Gama Bridge, the longest in Europe. From the River Tagus, Lisbon is dominated by the statue of Cristo Rei – Christ the King – with outstretched arms protecting the city. Close by the Tagus lies the Alfama, the oldest part of the city and boasting Lisbon's Cathedral and the castle of São Jorge.

In the mid-seventies, as a bachelor, I was usually to be found at the roulette tables of the Casino Barriere in Deauville, the favourite of the French elite; the Casino Le Croisette in Cannes, the Palatia in Baden – Baden – inspired by the Palace of Versailles; Monte Carlo, Venice, St. Moritz, Athens and London. During this one year 'career', I did not make a fortune, but I did have a very healthy income.

This comparatively short career, I called my 'Playboy of the Western World' period.

On this particular evening, I was having a reasonable run of the tables in Estoril, the inspiration for the book and film 'Casino Royale', when I became aware of a tall, striking young blonde peering over my shoulder.

"I don't really understand roulette," she admitted with a captivating smile.

"It's really quite simple. Please, take some of my chips and play. The round ones - not the square ones," I added just in time.

I usually play a split: a two and four number and two-line system, moving around the table. Any number coming up within the area covered will show a profit. I find the odds more to my liking. To my consternation, she placed all the chips on number nineteen.

Easy come, easy go.

It came in.

"No, please, they're your winnings."

"I couldn't possibly – I was playing with your chips."

Despite all my protestations, she refused to keep her winnings. We compromised with a bottle of Dom Perignon, and lunch in Lisbon the following day.

Finding a small, traditional restaurant off the Avernida da Liberdada, I set out to impress her with my knowledge of Portuguese (I have five phrases). I ordered what I thought was suckling pig. Over the vinho verde, she recounted her time as a model. I was not surprized – she was a doppelganger of Diana Rigg.

Our order arrived under a huge silver dome. The smiling waiter whipped off the cover with a theatrical flourish, revealing the biggest mound of cabbage I have ever seen, from which protruded several greyish-pink pig's trotters.

"I'm so sorry," she confided, leaning forward over the table, "but I just can't eat them."

'Don't worry about it – neither can I."

'The model' headed for the exit while I left a large tip with the bill, with the excuse that we had a plane to catch.

Several years, and two offspring later, to add to her three daughters from a previous marriage, my wife 'the Model', read in 'The Times' St. Valentine's Day columns, a simple message:

'M: Pig's trotters, boiled cabbage and number nineteen: B'.

I presume we were the only two readers who had any idea what the message meant.

★ ★ ★ ★

Portugal's Algarve has the best all-round climate in Europe, with more days of sunshine than the State of California, and boasts 100 miles of coastline from Cape St. Vincent to the Spanish border in the east.

I had accepted a commission from a lifestyle magazine to write 'Christmas in the Algarve' and duly decamped for a villa in Vilamoura, our ensemble consisting of my wife, 'the Nurse' – please keep up - her three offspring and an 'adopted daughter' in her twenties. The intention was to have a festive season we would never forget.

Unfortunately, we succeeded.

Although the majority of visitors see only the airport at Faro, the city itself warrants a little time. Most of Faro was built after the earthquakes of 1532 and 1755; the old part of the city is still surrounded by its 9th Century Roman walls. Its open square was once the Roman forum and now has the 17th Century Cathedral and the Episcopal Palace. The 'golden church' of *Nossa enharado Carmois* is reputably the finest example of gold-leaf ornamentation in the

Algarve, its chapel walls lined with the bones of over 1200 monks.

The travails began as soon as we reached the villa and began unpacking.

"The villa's too small!"

"There's no pool!"

"The television's in Portuguese!"

"I'm not sharing a bedroom with anyone!"

"I want a bathroom to myself!"

"I wanted to stay at home for Christmas!"

"Why haven't we got a car?"

Faced with a mutiny of collective pique and curled lower lips, I 'phoned and ordered a rental car, then headed for the bar, on what was to prove the first visit of many.

I hoped next morning that everyone would be at least a little happy to be on holiday. Then it rained. And rained. And rained.

The brand new silver Renault Laguna rental car arrived.

"Why couldn't we get a convertible?"

"Because it's persisting down – now get in the car!"

To get everyone into the holiday spirit, I drove along the Algarve, west to Albufeira. Once a small fishing village with a castle, it became another casualty of the 1755 earthquake. Some of Albufeira's character and charm can still be found in its ancient alleyways. It has grown to become the tourist capital of the Algarve, with its 23 beaches and innumerable bars, restaurants and nightclubs. Or, according to my wife's adopted daughter: "Worse than Blackpool!"

Another satisfied customer.

I suggested lunch. With unerring accuracy, I chose the restaurant with salmonella on the menu. After lunch, I was the only one affected. As we reached the summit of the climb back to where I had left the car overlooking the town, I leaned over a low wall and re-examined my lunch. A passing family of English holidaymakers just had to make a comment.

"Disgusting – and it's only early afternoon!"

Albufeira not having been a great success, I suggested we drive inland to Silves. Set above the River Arade, it boasted the finest castle on the Algarve. Its city walls, arched bridges and Gothic Cathedral were well worth the drive.

Wisely, for dinner we ordered the signature dish of the Algarve: *Ameijohas na Cataplana,* the *cataplana* being the Islamic copper 'pressure cooker' in which is cooked and served baby clams, ham, sausage, onion, tomatoes, garlic, paprika and white wine.

Christmas Day morning. This particular year we had embargoed any presents costing more than one pound, based on the fact one offspring suffered from Compulsive Obsessive Disorder and the other two from permanent penury. The presents were duly given out. No-one even attempted to look grateful.

The only highlight of the festive season was Christmas Lunch at the Marina Hotel in Vilamoura. The food ran the gamit of the gourmand's A to Z: lobster, crab, crevettes, prawns, various fish, squid, octopus, mussels, oysters and clams; suckling pig, lamb, beef, veal, rabbit, chicken, game, and ham. The only complaint was from the eldest, the medical student.

"I refuse to eat the seafood – it reminds me of specimens I've dissected."

I noticed he had no medical problem with the champagne.

"And, this veal doesn't taste like veal – and it's the wrong colour."

"I'm not surprized – it's lamb."

He blamed the restaurant's diffused lighting.

I complimented the waiter on his English.

"It is better than your Portuguese, that's for sure."

This wasn't a problem – I didn't intend leaving a big tip anyway.

★ ★ ★ ★

On Boxing Day, we decided to counteract the effects of the previous day with a trip north to

Monchique, sitting between Foia and Picota, with its steep cobbled streets and dark alleyways. The neglected Franciscan Monastery is the ideal panoramic viewpoint for a photo shoot before visiting the town's 16th Century church.

As we left Monchique, we drove into a vertical curtain of torrential rain. As we drove ever higher up the winding mountain road, it became a monsoon. In the dense fog and low cloud, visibility was down to an arm's length, if one had very short arms, as we came to a stop on the summit. In fine weather, I did not doubt the views were spectacular. By now, it was difficult to see the bonnet of the car. Leaving the shelter of the car and braving the downpour, I attempted to see if we had enough road to turn the car around. It was then I noticed the tyre was flat. I explained everyone would have to get out of the car, into the fog and rain, while I changed the wheel. I only put the tyre iron down for a minute.

Suddenly, out of the mist, appeared 'The Hound of the Baskervilles'. Jet-black, size-wise it looked as if it should be wearing a saddle. Without breaking step, it seized the tyre iron in its jaws and disappeared back into the dense fog. Even though we adopt rescue dogs, I would cheerfully brain that animal with the tyre iron given half a chance.

No-one was carrying a mobile phone. We inched our way back down the mountain in first gear, wobbling on the flat tyre, and back to the civilization – and garage – of Monchique. So much for a stress-free day.

As I was here, I reminded the entourage, to work, between Christmas and New Year, we would be driving the whole coast from east to west in easy stages, returning to the villa each evening for dinner. To stock up on food, we paid an early morning visit to the fish market of Quarteira. Entering the indoor market, you are assailed by the smell of the sea and salt of the morning's catch and the strident calls of the fishwives at their stalls. Selecting one, we delighted the fisherman's wife by buying a huge, whole sea bass, and two kilos each of crevettes and fresh sardines. When she told us the cost we knew why she was so delighted. Sea bass steaks, crevettes and sardines, cooked in various ways, were on the menu each day, with salads, fresh bread and wine. After three days, we faced a mutiny. The 'gang of four' made it clear that, no matter how much it had cost, they were 'fished out'. Back to piri-piri chicken and French fries.

Ingrates.

★ ★ ★ ★

Taking the main dual carriageway east, we headed for the town of Tavira near the Spanish border. Built on two hills either side of the River Gilao, Tavira well deserves its repute as 'The Rome of the Algarve'. As 'the Nurse' is really into monastic and church history, and Tavira has twenty-two churches, it was a long day.

The next morning saw us heading west to the town of Lagos, in 1445 Europe's first slave market. Like so much else in the Algarve, its palace had been destroyed in the 'Great Earthquake'. It is now noted for its designer shops, beaches and coves, its 17th Century 'gold' church of Santo Antonio, and a museum of the region's odd finds – some very odd indeed.

On the westernmost promontory of the Algarve lies Sagres, south of Cape St. Vincent, the site of Henry the Navigator's fortress and School of Navigation. The English know it better as the scene of the sea battle of 1797, which resulted in Nelson's promotion to Admiral.

For our final foray, we decided upon Portimao, between Albufeira and Lagos, at the mouth of the River Arade. Founded by the Cathagnians, by the 6th century it was known as Pontus Hanibalis, after the Roman general Hannibal Barca. With its history as a major trading post, it came as no surprize to find it had traded with the province of Britannia, particularly Cornwall. Over the centuries, Portimao became a haven for smugglers and pirates, known as the Algarve's shopping centre, it has little else to recommend it, the only exception being the town's church, dating from 1476 and renovated in 1717. The town's council's obsession with progress resulted in most buildings of historical interest being demolished.

We did not see much of Portamao. We saw a lot of the Regional Police Headquarters. We had been crossing the dual carriageway when we were hit by an old, 'corrugated iron' Renault full of Germans. I decided they had either come down the dual carriageway at one hell of a speed, or the Second World War had restarted and we hadn't been told.

When the police arrived, the young Germans became extremely vocal. I pleaded an impending coronary. The next several hours were spent in the Police Headquarters giving statements. Unaware of my German being fluent, I listened as the occupants of the Renault explained how I had come out of nowhere and rammed their car at high speed. That would have been quite an achievement given I was crossing the dual carriageway in first gear at five miles per hour.

The entire front of our Laguna was no more. It had ceased to be. Or, at least, it was strewn across the Portimao dual carriageway. As darkness fell, the police told us we could go, returning our documents and car keys. As we rattled and shook our way out of the police compound, we left a trail of various car parts in our wake. The English Traffic Police would have immediately judged the car un-roadworthy.

The journey back to Vilamoura seemed to take three weeks. What was left of the remaining headlight was intent upon scanning the night sky in case of an air raid. We drew unwanted attention from pedestrians and motorists, especially passing police patrols.

The next morning, I telephoned the manager of the car rental office. He was not impressed. After coming out to inspect the car, he refused to exchange it, and suggested we only drive in daylight.

"No," I explained. "we need a new car – this one's broken."

I asked myself what else could possibly go wrong.

Silly question.

★ ★ ★ ★

I collapsed in a heap, with a temperature only a little less than the surface of the sun. I could not keep even a glass of water down. The 'adopted daughter' then collapsed in sympathy. 'The Nurse' ordered us both to our bedrooms, with an order not to even attempt to get up.

Next morning, I stumbled from my bed, absolutely naked (not a pretty sight), to yet again attempt to make it to the bathroom. As I opened my bedroom door, there stood the maid.

She screamed.

I screamed.

She dropped her mop and bucket and fled. I spent the rest of the day waiting for the Portuguese Vice Squad.

New Year's Eve. At five to midnight, I staggered downstairs to join 'the Nurse'. Everyone else was out partying, with the exception of the 'adopted daughter', who was upstairs hallucinating.

As Portuguese television showed London's Trafalgar Square at midnight, we shared a bottle of champagne to let in the New Year. I then crawled back up the stairs, and remained comatose until the return flight.

Thank God for small nurses.

Comparatively recently, we had cause to return to the Algarve. This time not on a press trip, but to eldest offspring's wedding. As he and his bride,and several guests, were qualified doctors, at least I could be sure of medical attention should I need it. The wedding took place at a clifftop spa resort. The resort was fine. It was the 'designer cobbled' paths and roads which caused a problem. This trip, I had actually arrived in a wheelchair. Cobbles are definitely disabled unfriendly. My every bone vibrated.

Wheelchair to baggage store. As I walk, with the aid of a cane and a nurse, three times slower than the average wedding guest, I missed a lot. I arrived at the pre-wedding cocktail party minutes after it had closed down.

The groom had dispersed the sixty-odd guests between several rented villas, some distance from the resort. Directions in the Algarve are given simply as GPS co-ordinates. Problem: the taxis had not got GPS.

'The Nurse' decided to head over to one of the rented villas, to see her daughter and grand-daughter, ordering a taxi at reception. Handing the duty manager the destination co-ordinates texted by her daughter, she then spent the next 45 minutes waiting as he tried to make sense of the co-ordinates. Finally, he came up with the name of the villa, handing it to the taxi driver on his arrival. I got the distinct impression that GPS co-ordinates were a foreign country to him.

I opted to remain on the balcony of our villa and read.

Some hours later, she returned.

"Did you have a nice time?"

Her look I knew well. It could wither from 500 yards.

"Have a nice time? I haven't bloody *been* anywhere!"

Over a stiff drink, her afternoon unfolded.

The taxi driver did not have GPS (surprize). He had taken over half an hour for what should have been a ten-minute journey. He had stopped and beamed with satisfaction, pointing to the villa in front of them. She compared it with the photo sent to her mobile by her daughter. It bore no resemblance to the one she was looking at. Logically, she attempted to call her daughter for directions. It had been then she had discovered that her server had not transferred her mobile to the Portuguese network. Handing her mobile to the driver, she had pointed to the photo of the villa.

The next three hours had been spent driving around the western Algarve in ever-decreasing circles, looking for the elusive villa. Finally, they had given up, both teetering on the verge of a nervous breakdown, and driven back to the resort.

I might possibly have found the saga slightly amusing, had my wife not paid the taxi driver what was on the meter.

The wedding proved both simple and moving, conducted by the pastor the bride had flown out from her local church in London. The groom had flown in his favourite band for the reception, and a 'Wedding Planner' whom, from where I was sitting, seemed to think part of his responsibility was panic. The youngest sibling and her daughter were maids of honour. The second eldest was determined to enjoy himself, until the bar were instructed not to serve him any more alcohol – only fruit juice.

At the reception, the time came for the obligatory speeches. Unfortunately, the best man had written a short novel. Consequently, other speeches ran late. The resort's catering staff were signalling frantically from behind the hot buffet – which was cooling rapidly. It was necessary to bring down the curtain on speeches. I put my speech notes back in my pocket. This was no great loss. I had simply been going to welcome the bride into a totally dysfunctional family, and wish that all her travails would be small ones.

Chapter Six
Alligator Alley

Pressure of work for American media made it necessary to relocate there, initially to Florida and Palm Beach island – 'Millionaires Playground'. It remains the only place where I have seen a Ferrari in a 'garage sale'. To the majority of tourists, Florida *is* Orlando. I have to admit, I have been known to check out the rides at Disneyworld and Universal Studios, if I can borrow a friend's child as my 'cover'. Only 20 minutes from Orlando is the 7,000 acre Wekiwa Springs State Park, at Apopka. On my visit, I intended canoeing up the Wekiwa River, and checked the route with a Park Ranger.

"Your choice, sir," he pointed at the river. "The water's warmer than usual, so it's attracted the 'gators further downstream."

He went on to point out that alligators can jump out of the water, landing on top of your canoe – and you. I had no intention of becoming a floating lunch. As they could not provide a steel, four-foot-sided canoe with machine-gun posts front and aft, I decided I'd give canoeing a miss.

Palm Beach is an island which strives to keep its distance from its mainland neighbours, separated by the Inland Waterway. West Palm Beach and Lake Worth were originally developed simply to service Palm Beach. Access to the island is by three bridges: the Southern Boulevard, Royal Oak and Flagler Memorial, all monitored around the clock by the island's own Police Department, to keep out 'undesirables'. A photo ID card, showing your address as being on Palm Beach itself, can give an impression of affluence. A false impression in my case.

Sixteen miles long, and the easternmost town in Florida, Palm Beach has an average resident age of 67 and 97% of residents are white. It was voted 'America's Best Place to Live' – they forgot to add 'if you can afford it'. The island's motto is 'The Best of Everything'. I never did determine if the motto meant they wanted the best of everything or already had it.

The year-round population is only some 10,000, but the arrival of the 'snowbirds' –

northerners escaping the winter – easily triples that figure.

A road sign you do not see in England is 'Evacuation Route'. With ten hurricanes in less than a century, it is as well to know your escape route. In summer, when the snowbirds have flown back north, there is little traffic, the residents enjoying the return to peace and quiet. One would imagine it would be safe to drive on the island. Wrong. Many drivers are in their eighties and above, with the resultant deterioration of reflexes and eyesight. The most common accident in Palm Beach is the fender-bender, in English, a rear-ender.

I was on my sundeck when I heard the impact. Within minutes, the police and ambulance arrived. A positive of living on an island is the rapid response times.

"Anything interesting?' I asked the police officer, making sure he glimpsed the Palm Beach address on my Press ID card.

"Nah, just another fender-bender – lady in her nineties."

I had noticed the paramedics busily applying neck and spinal braces, defibrillator and readying a body hoist.

"Well," I turned back to the police officer, "it looks pretty serious from where I'm standing."

"The rear end impact was only around ten miles an hour," he explained, "but it shattered just about every bone in her body. Guess it comes with the age – she just crumbled."

I did a lot of walking on Palm Beach island.

It is certainly the most surreal place I have ever lived.

The town was established in 1896 by Henry Morrison Flagler, founder of Standard Oil, and property and railroad mogul who had made the coast accessible by train. He built two luxury hotels: The Royal Poinciana and The Breakers, the latter, with its Renaissance Revival architecture, is listed on the US National Register of Historic Places, and still a Palm Beach institution.

During my residency, the Breakers tennis pro' was Chris Evert Lloyd. Unfortunately, this did nothing to improve my backhand. I couldn't keep my mind on the game.

The highlight of the year is the Palm Beach 'Season', when the island returns to the Edwardian Era; the 'coming out' of debutantes is alive and well in Palm Beach. In the pillared mansions of the rich (old money) and famous (new money) cocktail parties abound, as do numerous charity dinners at $1,000 a plate. I cannot for the life of me recall if the International Red Cross Ball was white tie and the Palm Beach Opera party black tie, or vice versa. One of the venues at which one must be seen socially is the Palm Beach Polo Club, preferably in a private box. The highlight was the Rolex Trophy match playing HRH Prince Charles and his team, the return match being the Dorchester Trophy, sponsored by the hotel's owner, the Sultan of Brunei, played at Windsor Great Park.

An acquaintance whose business ethics were suspect, suffered from a complete lack of sartorial co-ordination. His PA had taken control of his wardrobe, labelling and numbering his clothes into sets comprising shoes, socks, trousers. shirt and tie and jacket. After a carefully-planned evening involving his PA in a shot drinking contest, we persuaded her to change all the labels at random.

The next evening, he joined us at a casual dress cocktail party, wearing grey shoes, luminous orange socks, canary yellow slacks, purple shirt with green tie and a powder blue jacket.

We all told him he looked great.

One particular Sunday was almost my last.

I had driven over to Lake Worth Lagoon for lunch on the mainland. I ordered an ice tea. The waitress asked me if I wanted regular or Long Island iced tea. Presuming they were similar, I ordered the Long Island. What I was not aware of, was this iced tea contained every alcoholic spirit known to man.

That is how I came to run a red light.

I was driving a red sports convertible, top down, and the top of the traffic police's hit list. Suddenly, I was in a roadblock of four police cars. I turned off the engine, which also killed the quad' stereo system, and stepped from the car. Evidently, due to the volume of the music, I had not heard the order: "Stay in your vehicle!"

As I stepped out, they drew their weapons and took aim. On me.

"Hands on your head – now!"

No problem.

"On the ground – now!"

Even less of a problem.

The handcuffs were extremely tight. Once we reached the station, they were removed, and I was put in the 'holding cage'. My fellow prisoners were one youth, stoned, and extremely nervous; the other, a huge black guy, six foot four and built like a brick outhouse, with muscles on his muscles. He was the opposite of nervous. It took several phone calls to spring me – proving the adage it's not what you know, but who you know…

One of the most impressive estates on the island is Mar A Lago. Built by Wall Street broker, E. F. Hutton, for his wife Marjorie Merriweather Post, the cereal heiress, with its 58 bedrooms, 33 bathrooms, a ballroom and 6 tennis courts and pool. Following her death, it was bought by the billionaire Donald Trump, at below market value for cash. Thus began the 'Battle of the Flagpole'.

Trump had erected a tall flagpole on the ocean side of the estate, falling foul of Palm Beach Zoning Laws. A settlement was finally agreed. The flagpole was lowered by ten feet and moved further from the ocean. It also cost Trump $100,000 in donations to charity. In return, he dropped his $250,000 action against Palm Beach.

North of Palm Beach lies Lake Okeechobee, or 'Big Water', the largest freshwater lake in the southern USA. The Seminoles won a great victory at the Lake over the US Army in 1837. Noted for its nightclubs, it is imperative to carry photo ID. Even with a Zimmer frame and several great-grandchildren, they will still insist of proof of age.

It was just not my night.

"Oh, I just love your accent," said the 18-year-old blonde (I was between wives at the time), clutching her Tequila Sunrise. "Where y'all from?"

I knew from experience it would be a waste of time to say anything other than London. This time, even that did not help.

"Oh, London – tell me, is that in France?"

End of conversation.

I only once made the mistake of using the line: 'where have you been all my life?'

She pointed out she hadn't been alive during the first half…

Embarrassing.

In the course of interviewing a Seminole tribal elder, I asked

"I guess you make most of your income from the tourists, these days?"

"No," he smiled, "from our casino."

I suppose it beats wrestling alligators for a living.

One February weekend, two female friends (still a bachelor) and I decided to head across

Alligator Alley to the Pow-Wow, the Seminoles' Tribal Festival and Parade. The six tribes of the Seminole had been gradually pushed back into the Everglades, initially by Andrew Jackson in order to annexe Florida, in the First Seminole War of 1817. This had been followed by the next from 1835 to 1842. By the end of the Third Seminole War in 1859, over 4,500 Seminoles had been forced to live in the relative isolation of the Everglades.

Alligator Alley is really Interstate 95, running from Florida's south-east coast to Naples in the west. It had been opened in 1969 as a toll road, and still is. We drove the Alley with headlights on, mandatory because of the shimmering heat haze rising from the road. The road signs warn of 'Panther Crossing', as well as alligators crossing the road. They don't need to look both ways. Obviously, the top of my convertible was firmly up – I had no intention of becoming 'meals on wheels'.

The Seminole Tribal Festival is a celebration of their history and culture, and an opportunity to meet other tribes and barter goods. Apart from the tribal storytellers, musicians and traditional 'stomp' dancers, there are the traditional alligator wrestlers for the tourists. This involves dragging a full-size 'gator out of a mud pool by its tail, sitting on its back, opening its jaws and putting your head inside, and, hopefully, getting it out again before the 'gator's jaws snap closed like a steel trap. I resisted the invitation to join in, and instead, had a 'gator burger' for lunch.

At the end of the day, as we headed back over the Alley, one of my passengers said she knew a short cut. I knew I should never have listened. Within thirty minutes we were hopelessly lost and running out of petrol. Then we heard the shooting, and headed in that direction.

Bad move.

The trail opened onto a huge landfill site. Fifty plus 'rednecks' were blasting away at wooden cut-outs of the US Army, armed with every fully automatic weapon that could be bought – and some that couldn't. They began to shout and point in our direction. We reversed at speed. Later, I found we had stumbled across a contingent of the 'Southern Army', intent on the overthrow of the US Government.

We looked desperately for a sign to civilization – anything with a gas station. We found a hand-painted wooden sign pointing up a dirt track road. We took it. The small town was really that: eight ramshackle wooden buildings – but with a gas station. I say a gas station – it was really a pre-Second World War petrol pump. As we pulled up to the pump, the girls began to look nervous. Looking in my rear view mirror, I began to get nervous.

Walking slowly toward us were some twenty man and boys, all dressed in checked shirts, baseball caps and denim bib and brace overalls.

They did not look friendly. An unshaven baseball-capped local shuffled to the pump. His eyes seemed to say 'the lights are on, but there's nobody home'. I asked him to fill up the tank.

"Nope."

The 'townsfolk' were getting uncomfortably closer. The girls clung onto each other as I drove off – very fast. In my rear-view mirror, I could see the locals gathered in a silent group, watching us disappear into the distance.

Eventually emerging from the backwoods and finding a gas station – we were by now running on fumes – the girls relaxed.

"Where the hell was that?"

To me, the answer was obvious.

"Stephen King Country."

★ ★ ★ ★

On my way to 'God's Country', the south-west, I decided to look up an old friend in Las Vegas. Set in a basin in the Mojave Desert, and surrounded by the Sierra Nevada mountains, its name means 'the meadows', and was used as a stopover on the old Spanish Trail from Texas. My main memory of Dallas, Texas, is being trapped between floors in the hotel elevator until rescued by the Fire Department. The girl on reception could not understand why I was checking out.

A piece of useless trivia about Las Vegas will be unknown to female tourists: in the men's room at the Main Street Station, the urinals are set into a section of the Berlin Wall.

For some reason, Las Vegas is extremely popular with Hawaiians, over 3,000 visitors a week, found in the casinos of The Strip, better known as 'Glitter Gulch'.

In 1855, Nevada was annexed by the USA from Mexico and, with the railroad arriving in 1905, Las Vegas became a city in 1911. The year that ensured Las Vegas' future was 1931, when gambling was legalized in parts of Nevada. On Boxing Day, 1945, Bugsy Segal opened the Flamingo, on what was to become the four-mile Strip. Mega-casinos did not arrive until 1989, with The Mirage. When Howard Hughes bought up several casinos in the 1960s, it sounded the death knell of the mob's control of Las Vegas. The opening of the Hoover, or Boulder Dam, and the creation of Lake Mead in 1935, ensured a plentiful water supply and the growth of tourism.

The windows of the casinos are tinted black, so it is virtually impossible to tell if it is day or night outside. As I entered the casino, I was faced with a gigantic slot machine, containing $1,000,000 behind its bulletproof glass. As I checked in at reception, I was given one token to play. It was by this giant slot machine, that I witnessed one of the saddest scenarios I have ever seen. A young boy was lifted up by his father to put the token in the slot, and pull the handle. All hell broke loose: alarms, klaxons, music, flashing lights, bells and fanfares. He had won. The family went wild with joy.

Then, Casino Security arrived.

"I'm sorry sir, but we can't pay out. Nevada gambling laws state you have to be over twenty-one to gamble – and it was your son who played the slot."

The family frantically insisted it had been the father who played the machine.

"Sorry sir, but we have it all on CCTV."

Millionaires for five minutes. So near, and yet so far.

Enter T. D. 'Dean' Stoops, half-Cherokee horse whisperer and rodeo rider. His grandfather had broken horses for the 7th Cavalry. We had been friends in Cornwall until, suddenly one morning, he left his wife, threw his saddle over his shoulder and hitched north up the A30. When I met him I found out the reasons: the English climate and marriage. He was now working a small ranch outside Vegas, and living in a trailer. Meeting me at my resort hotel, he took full advantage of hot, running water. We drove out to the ranch, where my jaw dropped in surprize. There, in the middle of the arid desert, stood a white picket-fenced flower garden and lawn.

"Takes a helluva lot of water," he smiled, sheepishly. "I guess I stayed in England too long, huh?"

We sat with a cold beer, watching the sun go down over the desert. It was, sadly, the last time we would meet.

Dean had introduced me to a friend, the Head of Security at one of the major casinos. Their friendship was based on a mutual penchant for firearms – in Dean's case, a .44 Magnum. His friend offered me a tour of the casino. As he showed me one of the expensive 'high rollers' suites, he pointed to the huge bed.

"If you ever stay in a suite here, have a quiet night – know what I mean?"

"Why?" I asked naively.

He pointed at the ceiling.

"All the suites, especially the bedrooms, are filmed."

"Good God! Why?"

"Well, let's say somebody has to tell the senators and Congressmen how to vote."

I left it there.

★ ★ ★ ★

The journey from Las Vegas to Phoenix is worth the drive through the ever-changing vistas. I took Route 40, passing the Black Mountains and Kingman, to I95 at the Nevada – Arizona border. And on through the Halapai Valley Joshua Tree National Park, with a break at Wikieup (willow home) for rattler and fries in a basket. After lunch, onwards through the Weaver Mountains, past Alamo Lake and the Williams River; the desert drive past the Vulture Mountains and into the Valley of the Sun.

The majority of visitors to Arizona do not realize that only 15% is in private hands. The remaining 85% is comprised of Native American Reservations, National Parks and Recreation Areas. In fact, Arizona did not become the 48th State until 1912. Originally ceded after the American – Mexican War of 1847, it had been known as the Arizona Territory from 1863.

Phoenix lies in the Salt River Valley. Founded in 1868 at the confluence of the Salt and Gila rivers in the north-eastern Senoran Desert, it became a city in 1881. The coming of the railway and the advent of air conditioning secured its future development. The 1960s saw the growth of retirement communities such as Sun City, known locally as the 'Geriatrics Graveyard', and in the Valley, the growth of dude ranches and tourism. Temperatures between May to September can exceed 100°F for an average of 110 days, a climate similar to Riyadh; overnight lows plummet to 80°F. Even winter is usually 65°to 75°F – when residents break out the thermals.

Getting into travel writer mode, I set off to explore Arizona.

In the desert, boots are good. Sandals and flip-flops bad, bearing in mind rattlesnakes, sidewinders, scorpions, black widow spiders and gila monsters. I hate gila monsters. This Arizona desert lizard carries its venom in its jaws and, having sunk its teeth into your leg, grinds its teeth to release its poison. My desert guide told me that, even if you shoot off its head, it will carry on grinding. I prefer them as boots.

My destination was the 1,000 year-old ruins of a village of over 200 Hohokum, a Pima Indian word meaning 'those who have gone'. Their pit-houses were constructed by digging 2 to 3 feet underground, then building 5-foot adobe or stone walls. The skeleton poles were of bound Saguaro cactus and formed the corner posts and rafters; the roof was covered in branches and animal skins.

The Hohokum farmed the fertile flood plains of the Verde, Gila and Agua Fria rivers, growing corn, squash, beans, peas and Pima cotton for sandals and clothing. They also harvested the cactus when in season. Considered a delicacy, the cactus is still harvested by the Papago Indians.

An early settler predicted that, from the ashes of their civilization, a new one would arise as the phoenix from the ashes.

I was driving from Phoenix to Pinnacle Peak when the 'duster' hit. I got the top of the convertible up with seconds to spare, thanks to a warning on the car radio. Day became night, and traffic came to a standstill, as the red dust storm swept across the valley. That evening on Pinnacle Peak, a major desert lightning storm lit up the mountains as flashes of images in a silent film; the lightning strikes bounced from the tops of the saguaros. Only later did I discover this was considered a once in a lifetime experience.

The Pinnacle Peak Patio is famous for its steaks. I was about to find out another of its claims to fame. The waiter brought me the menu, then produced a large pair of scissors and cut off my tie, just below the knot.

"What the hell-" was as far as I got.

He explained house rules, posted at the entrance, warn anyone caught wearing a tie will have it snipped off by the scissor-wielding staff. He pointed at the ceiling. Hanging from the rafters were over 750,000 ties. This tradition had upset more than one tourist. I agreed. Me.

A two-pound medium rare porterhouse steak, cowboy beans, hot bread, salad and a pitcher of beer, eased my loss. Talking of beer: Pinnacle Pete had been a bucket-a-day mule. Finally, his liver gave out halfway through a bucket. His picket-fenced grave and headstone is in front of the restaurant.

Arizona: 'The Grand Canyon State'. My flight in a 4-seater Cessna from Scottsdale Airport flew at 1,000 feet over Cave Creek and Carefree, Cross Ranch, Rimrock, Sedona and Flagstaff, landing at the small Grand Canyon Airport on the South Rim. The canyon was formed by the Rio Colorado, or Red River – which is actually blue-green - and is 1 mile-deep, 18 miles wide and 227 miles in length, and formed an impenetrable barrier to the early Conquistadores. On the floor of the canyon is its only crossing point, the Rainbow Bridge. The sections of the bridge were carried down by mule. The Angel Trail, by burro, is still the only way down, and still delivers supplies to the Rainbow Ranch. The only other habitation in the canyon is the Navajo village, protected from tourism.

The first train to the Grand Canyon rim ran in 1901, heralding the demise of the stagecoach run. It was an easy choice for passengers: a whole day's dusty, choking, bone-jarring, cramped journey for $20, or a comfortable, 3-hour train journey for under $4. No contest.

18 miles south-east of Phoenix on I10 is Tucson, 60 miles north of Mexico, and Arizona's second city, situated in the Santa Cruz Valley in the Senoran Desert, surrounded by five

mountain ranges. It also, on my visit, had a crime rate four times the national average.

The child in me still enjoys a visit to Old Tucson: '12 miles and 100 years from town'. This western frontier town was originally built in 1939 for the William Holden film 'Arizona', but since, has been the location of literally hundreds of films and television series. Grab some chow and a cold beer at the saloon, then mosey down Main Street. The railroad station was used for the films 'Posse' with Kirk Douglas, and John Wayne's 'McClintock'. Down the street is the clapperboard schoolhouse from 'Little House on the Prairie'. The doorway of the Mission, is where John Wayne met his end in 'The Alamo'; the old barber's shop doubled as a stagecoach depot in several movies, including Paul Newman's 'Hombre'.

In the inevitable Madame Tussaud's are the waxwork figures of Geronimo and Cochise, and the Earps and Clantons from the gunfight at the OK Corral. Given the figures were modelled from the actual characters before or after death, they seem disappointedly short of stature and charisma. But, the same has been said about me.

Chapter Seven
Of Scams and Spooks

I n Israel, 5,000 years of history unfold. The country is some 48 miles long and 8 to 68 miles wide, with Eilat, the southernmost port in Israel, the tourist centre of the Red Sea. Rather than the teeming crowds and bustle of Eilat, I decided to base myself in Hof Almog, or Coral Beach, one of the world's premier diving centres, and within easy walking distance of Taba and the Egyptian border – were it not too hot to walk anywhere.

The temperature hit 110°F as we deplaned – rather like stepping from a fridge into a hot oven. Our accommodation was literally on Coral Beach, 30 seconds from the sea. It would have been fine had the air conditioning worked. It was cooler on the beach – in fact many guests preferred to sleep there.

Not one of my smartest choices.

From our balcony, the red mountains of Jordan over the water were reflected in the Sea parted by Moses, hence its name. It is advisable to drink at least three litres of water daily to avoid dehydration. I seem to do things in reverse. I am fine in the heat, but, as soon as I step into air conditioning, I look as if I have just stepped fully-clothed from a shower.

In the bank in Eilat, the small boy tugged at his mother's skirt.

"Mama! Mama! Look at the man over there – he's melting!"

A reasonably accurate description.

I knew my brief of 'Israel in a Week' would not be an easy one, given the number of places and sites on my 'hit list'. From the western coast of the Red Sea, northward through the Tunna Valley with its mushroom-like rock formations, site of the ancient copper mines and Pillars of King Solomon; through the heat of the barren Negev Desert to the mountain fortress of Masada, built on a plateau rising from the rock.

Built in 37BC by King Herod as a winter palace, it became the symbol of the Israelite resistance to Roman rule. The entire plateau was surrounded by a wall, reinforced with 37 towers, and containing an arsenal and a water supply from rainwater tanks, an aquaduct and quarters for 1,000 soldiers. Food was cultivated on the plateau and stored in warehouses. A seemingly impregnable mountain stronghold.

In 73AD, after the destruction of Jerusalem by the Romans, 1,000 Jewish zealots defended the plateau against the legions of the Roman General Flavius Siva for four long years. Finally, with inescapable military logic, the Romans simply built a ramp on the side of the plateau, the remains of which can still be seen. The defenders drew lots to kill each other rather than surrender; the last man standing to take his own life. The Romans recorded, from the total number of defenders, only two women and children were found alive.

As the symbol of Israel's fight for survival, each year recruits of the Tsanal – the Israeli Army – are sworn in and issued their weapons on the summit of Masada, swearing 'Masada will never fall again'.

Nearby, the ancient cities of Sodom and Gomorrah were destroyed by the same earthquake which turned the nearby freshwater lake into the Dead Sea of acids, minerals and salts in which no life can survive. The lowest point on Earth at 1296 feet below sea level, the Sea is 50 miles long and 10 miles wide.

With ten times the salt content of any other sea, it is impossible to sink or swim in its waters. The pictures of bathers floating on their backs while reading a newspaper are absolutely true. I tried it. It gives a weird sensation of being weightless. Its high concentrations of bromide, calcium, sodium and potassium, are used by the thermal health spa resorts by the Sea, as a supposed cure for skin diseases and respiratory problems.

Do *not* enter the Sea with any cuts or abrasions. 'The Nurse' (who should have known better) did. The miniscule cut on her ankle became painfully swollen and infected. It took several days of antiseptic dressings and a course of strong antibiotics before the inflammation was brought under control. Once your skin begins to sting, get out of the Sea and under the freshwater beach showers.

From this lowest point on Earth, begins the climb into the Judean Desert, passing Bedouin encampments with their goat herds, camels and 30-foot TV antenna. This particular day, they were watching reruns of 'Dallas'. In their tents, the men rest while the women work. Sounds like a workable system to me.

Journeying past the Mar Saba Monastery, where women are not permitted, we made a detour to the caves of Qumran. Here, in 1947, two Bedouin shepherds found seven jars of ancient manuscripts – The Dead Sea Scrolls. 600 fragments of the Isiah Scroll had been preserved. At the time of our visit, we were told over forty leopards had been counted in one night, hunting by a nearby village. Hardly the place to take an evening constitutional.

The River Jordan Valley is formed from springs running from the slopes of Mount Harmon. Running into the Dead Sea, it became contaminated, and was diverted to the north to provide freshwater for cultivation, and at a premium in a country comprised of two-thirds desert: The Negev, Judean and Samarian. Travelling by coach towards Jericho, past the Mount of Temptation – the reputed setting of Christ's confrontation with Satan – we ran into heavily-armed Israeli checkpoints. They confirmed that, for today, the road to Palestinian-controlled Jericho was 'open'.

The ancient city, conquered by Joshua in the 13th Century BC, had been rebuilt and expanded by Herod the Great. As Jericho was the main city of the Palestinians, we were warned to stay aware and not to give offence. Unfortunately, my wife's skirt was a little short by Palestinian standards and attracted attention and monetary offers. I'm not entirely sure she has forgiven me for haggling over the price.

Driving away from the ruins of the city, one of the coach windows was suddenly shattered by one of the flying bricks and stones, slightly injuring one passenger. We left to the sounds of anti-Israeli chants. One week later, the Israeli Government announced new measures were to be put in place 'in the interests of security'.

Motoring past Wadi Kelt, on to the Mount of Olives, with its panoramic view over the City of David, it is considered by many to be the centre of the Universe. The Mount of Olives cemetery is where, according to the prophets, the dead will be resurrected. The small stones, placed on the gravestones by relatives and friends, cannot be removed under Jewish law.

Jerusalem is a crossroads of different cultures, where Jews, Arabs, Muslims and Druse meet. Located within only a few hundred feet of the old city, are the most sacred sites of the three monotheistic religions: The Western or Wailing Wall, the Omar Mosque and the Holy Sepulchre, giving rise to 3,000 years of history and conflict. The view from the Mount of Olives is dominated, as is the city itself, by the golden dome of the Rock, or Omar Mosque, sacred to the Islamic religion. The Mosque was completed in 699AD, covering the Rock of Abraham, and the reason for Mohammed's journey from Mecca.

The Old City – the walled City of David – had been built on the site by Abraham, and became the Seat of Solomon. Time to send 'the Nurse' on a photo shoot by climbing up the walls of the Citadel and David's Tower. It is often overlooked by history that it's builder, King Herod, was renowned as an architect. It now houses a museum of the history of the city. The Old City is predominately the Arab Quarter; 35,000 Muslims make up one-third of the population. Its narrow streets and alleyways of market stalls and shops echo with the cries of vendors of carpets, brassware, jewellery, fabrics and spices; the fragrant aroma of wood and coffee mixing with the smell of falafel, the fried chickpea pastry of Arab cuisine. Negotiating the narrow streets, running the gauntlet of Arab boys with a range of wares, they lead to the Convent of the Scourging, the start of the Via Dolorosa, or 'Road of Sorrows'. The route follows the fourteen Stations of the Cross, in Jesus' footsteps from Pilate's Judgement Hall to Golgotha – the place of the skull – or Calvary Hill, the place of his crucifixion. The fourteenth, final station is Christendom's most sacred site, that of Jesus' tomb and resurrection, housed in its own chapel. This focal point of the Basilica of the Holy Sepulchre was built by the Crusaders on Byzantine foundations dating from the reign of Constantine the Great. The original Basilica was destroyed by Persian invaders in 514 AD.

The Basilica seems to have a marked and lasting effect on many visitors. During my visit, one young woman collapsed on the floor of the tomb in a seeming seizure. Her anguished cries could be heard reverberating around the Basilica.

"He's dead! He's dead! You killed Him! You killed the Son of God!"

The kind of reaction being not uncommon, three priests rushed over and made her as comfortable as possible where she lay, shouting and shaking uncontrollably.

What should have been controlled was the party of American tourists, who rushed over, cameras at the ready. Unbelievably, one of them pushed one of the priests out of his way.

"Hey – move your ass! Can't you see we're trying to film here!"

At the Dome of the Rock, it was not my day. The sacred site of Islam, where the footprints of the Prophet could be seen embedded in the Rock, was closed. It was the birthday of Mohammed, and open only to believers. As I said, even travel writers get it wrong.

At the foot of the Dome is the Western, or Wailing Wall.

The kotel Maaravi originally supported the Temple of Solomon, and is sacred to the Jewish people more than any other site. Since the time of the Roman occupation, the people of Israel have come to the Wall to pray, and demonstrate their sorrow over the destruction of the House of God. When Jerusalem was reunited in 1967, the structure concealing part of the Wall was torn down, creating the largest open-air synagogue in the world.

The Wailing Wall is segregated as the Orthodox Jewish religion does not allow men and women to pray together. I joined the men at their prayers, picking up a prayer shawl and cap at the entrance, as all heads must be covered. Two heads are better than one, so I sent 'the Nurse' off to join the women's enclave, which she found a very moving experience.

Several men were swaying backwards and forwards as they prayed, banging their foreheads into the wall. Looking at the resultant blood loss, I understood why a fax machine had been installed at the Wall as a less painful way of praying. All gain – no pain.

As usual, it was my fault.

I should have realized, had I a modicum of common sense, that photography was not exactly encouraged. By the wall stood a family group, engaged in part of the Barmitzvah, the ceremony which confirms a thirteen-year-old Jewish boy's coming of age and transition into adulthood. The proud father was holding a large, ornate scroll of the Torah, the first five books of the Bible. All the other men present were wearing small, black boxes strapped around their forehead, containing scraps of the Torah. I thought this was a great photo opportunity.

As all the male family members came towards me with baleful glares, I did the logical thing. I ran.

Heavily armed Israeli Defence Forces provided a highly visible presence at the Western Wall and in the Arab Quarter – a reminder of the fragile peace existing in the 'unified' city.

Bethlehem, the birthplace of Christ, lies six miles from Jerusalem. Should He be contemplating a second coming, He may wish to change the venue.

I have always said 'there is nothing like a good lunch'. Ours was nothing like a good lunch. Taken in a restaurant next to the Mary and Joseph Fish and Chip Shop (no, I'm not joking) in Manger Square, the undercooked shashlik was instant food poisoning. I hadn't had such a good time since I contracted an acute case of food poisoning from a curried goat on a beach at Port Au Prince on Haiti. The only justifiable reason for visiting Bethlehem is the Church of the

Nativity, reputably the site of the stable where Christ was born.

'Hic de Verine Maria Jesus nata est':

'Here from the Virgin Mary Jesus was born'.

In single file, down a steep set of steps, lies the crypt. Set into the floor is the silver star and altar marking the place of His birth. Tour groups of all nationalities, must join a long queue and be pushed and prodded like cattle on a humid, airless staircase.

Being English, it just had to be the French. Their tour guide looked remarkably like David Suchet as Hercule Poirot, and was stood directly behind me on the steps. He continuously and 'accidently' prodded me between the shoulder blades with the point of his pink parasol. He turned to address his tour group.

"My apologies, but we shall soon be where we wish to be – as soon as these stupid, ignorant English get out of our way."

I am normally a very patient person. I can only put it down to the humidity and lack of oxygen. Turning – which was not easy on those stairs - with noses nearly touching, I explained in carefully chosen French, that we had not stopped on the stairs for a picnic. I also explained exactly what I would do with his parasol if he did not cease and desist with the prodding. By a hair's breadth, I escaped being the only Englishman ever to be arrested for inciting a riot in the Church of the Nativity, Bethlehem.

Back in England for Christmas, we went to our local church' carol service.

"We shall now sing 'O, Little Town of Bethlehem'."

Oh, no we shan't. I sang an entirely different version:

"O, little town of Bethlehem, how still we see thee lie, waiting for the tourist coach to bring their shekels by..."

Apart from 'the Nurse', who prodded me in the ribs with her elbow, I don't think anyone noticed.

The return southwards was via Be'er Sheba – or it should have been. I discovered my new white, designer jacket was still hanging in the wardrobe of our room at the hotel in Jerusalem. I had a word with the driver. I should perhaps point out at this juncture, that we were the only English on a coach crammed with Germans. As usual, they were blissfully unaware I understood German. So was the coach driver. He grabbed his microphone and announced:

"Thanks to the stupid Englander, we now have to return to the hotel in Jerusalem to retrieve his jacket. This means we shall be late back in Eilat."

Germanic heads turned as one. I now know the meaning of the phrase: 'If looks could kill'. They shouted at the driver:

"Our holiday is all inclusive – we had better not be back late for dinner – it is paid for!"

We were horrendously late back to their hotel.

Shame.

★ ★ ★ ★

Having completed the 500-mile round-trip, the temperature in Coral Beach had plummeted to a mercifully cool 90°. I have dived and snorkelled my way from the Maldives to Tahiti, but the Red Sea is superlative for close-up marine life. We spent the remaining days swimming with the sergeant major fish, turkey fish, the Red Sea starfish, octopus and giant devil ray. I drew the line at socializing with the Black Tail Sharks. I prefer the sea to turn red due to the sunset.

On the final evening, I decided on a romantic candlelit dinner for two on the wooden terrace of a restaurant by the marina. When we ordered the red mullet and prawns, we had not an inkling we would be dining free of charge. When the credit card voucher came to the table I signed (pre-keypad), then noticed they had forgotten to include the wine. They duly returned with a new slip to sign.

Sometime later, back in the UK, my credit card statement showed us having four dinners, at the same time, on the same evening at the same restaurant. After several attempts to call-in the restaurant's voucher copies, my credit card company informed me they were removing all the restaurant's charges from my account.

Dinner would have tasted so much better had I known it was free.

★ ★ ★ ★

Dhiveli Raajjah: The Maldives. 145 miles southwest of Sri Lanka in the Indian Ocean, comprised of 1,192 small *fushis,* or islands, with reefs forming 26 atolls. As a country, less than a third is dry land. Only 202 islands are inhabited, the smallest having a population of three females. Of the 300,000 population, 70,000 are foreign workers and 33,000 illegal immigrants.

The Maldives, remarkably, was known to very few tourists until the early 70s. In 1972 the first two resorts, Bandos Island and Kurunba, opened. Today, there are around 90 resorts and 600,000 tourists each year, with tourism accounting for 60% of foreign exchange receipts as the country's main industry.

Arriving at the capital, Malé, we were transferred by launch to our fushi and a beach bungalow by the lagoon, traditionally built with pine interior, veranda and *gifili* – a bathroom with an open-air shower. The bungalow also came with its own *gecko,* a small, harmless lizard. As far as I am concerned when travelling, the more the merrier – they eat mosquitos.

The local language – Dhivehi – is Sanskrit, Pashto and Persian based. For just a few basic phrases try *Haalu Kihineh?*: How are you?, *Shaknyyan:* Thank you; *Baajja yeri hendhuneh:* Good morning, and *Vakivelanee:* Goodbye. As with any country, they really appreciate that you have made the attempt. The resort staff grapevine gave out the news there was an Englishman who actually spoke Dhivehi – very, very basically, I hasten to add. The management sent our houseboy, Abdullah, to invite me to worship at their mosque. I had to explain I was not a Muslim. Interestingly, non-Muslims cannot vote in the Maldives.

Sat on our veranda, I noticed one of the staff gathering up fallen coconuts, then shinning up the palm trees to machete those which looked about to fall. It was not unknown for a falling coconut to brain an unsuspecting tourist. I called him over and offered him a dollar for a coconut, which he opened with his machete. From then onwards fresh coconut milk became a morning ritual.

The thatched-roofed beach restaurant, by the edge of the lagoon, served a consistently high standard of Maldives cuisine. However, there was another bar, which appeared to cater for those who were on an all-inclusive holiday, and determined to get their money's worth.

Cue scam.

The bar relied on the heavy drinkers to have alcoholic amnesia the next morning. As a travel writer, I like to think I know most of the 'holiday scams', and this one was no exception, well-tried and tested worldwide. As we took a table for a cold drink, one of the bar staff greeted us with a smile.

"Sir, you forgot to settle your bar tab when you left last night."

The bill was for six beers.

"I think we have a problem," I smiled. His smile disappeared. "I do not, and never have used your bar. Secondly, for medical reasons, I am not allowed to drink beer. Bring your Bar Manager – now!"

"Sorry! Sorry! Is mistake." pleaded the Bar Manager. It certainly was. "Look – I tear up bill – okay?"

"Okay," I replied," just as conjecture, let's say you get a half-dozen guests to sign a bill each day, how much do you make when you share out the kitty at the end of the week?"

I happened to mention this when talking to one of the main tour operator's representatives.

"Oh shit! They're at it again!"

Evidently, the previous season, the bar staff had even loaded these fictitious bills onto every travel companies' rep's accounts. It was, and I presume still is, a standard scam.

On the beach, I came upon a rather strange signpost. Its wooden-arrowed pointers showed the distance to the various cities of the world. London was noticeable by its absence. However, it did show Glasgow as being 8,963 km away. Really interesting information if you happen to come from Glasgow.

The next day proved to be 'travails day' – and painful. We decided to go our separate ways, 'the

Nurse' to the Try Dive, and myself to the Spa for a foot, neck and full body massage. Both proved equally disastrous. At only one fathom deep, 'the Nurse' was forced to give up the dive due to severe pain in the ears, which she correctly diagnosed as an inability to equalize pressure in the inner ear. The end of dreams of scuba diving.

Meanwhile, back at the massage spa, my young, attractive masseuse had finished the relaxing foot and neck massage.

Then she walked up my spine.

I think they probably heard my screams of pain in Colombo.

It was my own fault. I had neglected to mention I had three compacted vertebrae and a crushed disc. I had to assure the gathered manager and staff, I did not hold them legally responsible, as demonstrated with a large tip. I walked with a limp for the next three days.

We took a small boat reef cruise which was to certainly prove to be unusual. Upon arrival in the Maldives, I had interviewed a leading political activist, whose avowed mission was to bring down, as he saw it, the corrupt government, and restore democracy. (This was before the time of the current President, I hasten to add). During the course of the interview, he explained to me that his friend, an attorney, had announced his intention of standing as presidential candidate in the forthcoming election. That evening he had taken his boat out on a night fishing trip. He was never seen again.

We had been followed for the past 48 hours. When we boarded the boat, our shadow followed, seating himself within earshot. He tried to the best of his ability to find the horizon fascinating. Unfortunately for him, all the male passengers were in shorts and plain shirts or tee shirts in subdued colours. His garish Hawaiian shirt and long trousers, with brogue shoes, could not have been called low profile. He really needed to get out more. If he was Maldives' intelligence, then he desperately need a refresher course in tradecraft – particularly surveillance.

Halfway through the cruise, a sudden squall blew up, the precursor of a storm. Sensibly, the Captain made the decision to head back to the island. The small boat was pitching and rolling heavily, passengers hanging on to the roof canopy's struts. Several passengers were badly affected, hanging over the boat's side, including our minder. Unfortunately, no-one had told him never to vomit *into* the wind...

He was violently ill for the remainder of our dash for the shore, and the first out of the boat. We never saw him again.

In the warm, shallow turquoise lagoon, I was doing my usual impression of a sitting Buddha, when my better half pointed and asked "What's that?"

'That' was a shark. I broke the Olympic record for getting out of the water. It may have only been a foot long, but in my book a shark is a shark. 'The Nurse' had an even closer encounter with the fully-grown variety while snorkelling at the north end of the island, after dark. As I have tried for years to point out to her, after dark, the smaller fish come in to feed; the larger fish come inshore to eat the smaller fish, and the sharks, to feed on the larger fish. This food chain applies worldwide, from the Indian Ocean to the Pacific.

My closest encounter had been off Grand Bahama. A Canadian friend and myself had taken a pedalo out to sea. Unfortunately, we got caught in a strong cross current. No matter how fast we paddled, we were getting nowhere, and were drifting ever further from the shore.

Then the dorsal fin appeared. It was a big shark. It was a very big shark. It began circling the pedalo.

"What do you think we should do?" asked my Canadian friend.

"Well, I don't know about you, but I'm getting my feet the hell out of the water."

I remembered reading somewhere, that the shark is likely to mistake your feet for fish. I was more than aware that, if the shark came up beneath the fibre-glass pedalo, we'd be thrown into the water as a buffet lunch. The only other relevant advice I had read, said 'punch the shark as hard as possible on its nose. This will confuse it for five milliseconds – then it'll be mad as hell.'

Luckily, the lifeguards of the Grand Bahamas Hotel and Country Club, monitor the pedalos through binoculars. The high-powered motor launch reached us in minutes, one of the lifeguards carrying a rifle, and towed us back to the shore. We spent the rest of the afternoon in the bar, our rescue from the jaws of death being worth several drinks.

We spent the next day snorkelling in the deep-water reefs, where you can swim with Imperial Wrasse, turtles, manta and stingrays, and dolphins. That evening, we decided to join friends for dinner on the deck of the floating restaurant. We ordered the shrimp and lobster bisque, red snapper, and white and red wine. As the first course arrived, the heaven's opened – a tropical rainstorm. It was the first and only time we have dined under the protection of several large golf umbrellas, held, for the duration of the meal, by absolutely sodden waiters. Now *that* is what I call customer service.

Taking a seaplane from its pontoon, looking down at the atolls, surrounded by turquoise lagoons, one can see it change to the deep blue of the ocean beyond the reefs; a shimmering necklace of precious stones set in the Indian Ocean. It would be sad to think on 'Paradise Lost', but, unfortunately, it is a fact that the Maldives could disappear for ever. The problem lies in global warming. None of the atolls are more than 5 feet above sea level, many considerably less, and at the mercy of rising sea level.

A 'Safari Cruise', on a 24-foot schooner, is a good way to lose a straw hat. Mine blew overboard in a sudden gust of wind. The Captain asked me if he should put about and retrieve it. I explained I never really liked the hat anyway, for which he was truly grateful.

Ten minutes later, one of the teenage girl passengers lost her plastic sun visor over the side. She stridently insisted that the schooner turn around to look for it. The Captain did so, and the crew gaffed her sun visor from the water. That was when we found we were firmly aground on a coral reef. It took almost an hour to re-float the schooner. The Captain was definitely not amused – especially when the girl complained about the delay.

Dolphins acted as our pilots as we cleared the reef into open ocean. Shipboard lunch could not have been fresher, caught off the stern some ten minutes earlier. Hoisting the sails, we continued out into the now dark blue waters for deep reef snorkelling, followed by tanning time on a partially exposed sandbank.

The atolls are ruled by *Atholu Venyaa,* or chiefs, appointed by the President. Tourist resorts are not allowed on the islands with native inhabitants – in fact contact is discouraged. For some strange reason, whilst on an atoll, they sat 'the Nurse' in a wicker armchair and carried it into the lagoon, followed by a short ceremony declaring her *kateeb,* or Chief, of the island.

As, in reality, it was a sandbank which disappeared with the tides, I could only presume it was a part-time position.

I had made the mistake of speaking in *Dhivehi* to the Captain, when my straw hat had blown off into the ocean. This had resulted in chats with all the crew, and copious refills of red wine as they vied with each other to pour it. The Captain presented me with his own copy of a Dhivehi – English Dictionary.

I must admit, in retrospect, the return voyage was just a little hazy.

Chapter Eight
Crap Soup and a Concierge

F ragrant Harbour: the richest jewel in the British Crown, thanks to the First Opium War with China in 1842. This was to force opium on the Chinese people, not to eradicate its use. The British Empire thrived on trade, and this was no exception. Ostensibly a collection of fishing villages, the Treaty of Nanking secured the future of Hong Kong, with the Kowloon Peninsular being ceded to the British in 1860, followed by a 99 lease in 1898 of the New Territories.

Lying at the mouth of the Pearl River, with an area of 425 miles, the Hong Kong of my time there, was prior to the official handover (or should that be handback) to the Peoples Republic of China on 30 June, 1997. Having said that, very little has changed. Girding its loins to become the world's new financial and economic superpower, the PRC are more than aware of the value of Hong Kong as an international financial centre, and are not about to rock the sampan.

One change I welcomed with open arms was the building of the new Lantau International Airport. Hong Kong's old airport was one of the hairiest landings on the planet. Literally approaching between high-rise residential blocks, one could look out of the plane window and see what the Chinese families in their apartments were watching on television, or having for dinner. The chances of overshooting the runway into the sea was always uppermost on one's mind when landing. It had always been a temptation to take a snorkel, fins and a mask as carry-ons.

Once the handover decision was made public, there was an immediate flurry of financial activity. Many an asset was converted into gold and international currencies and transferred out of Hong Kong. The majority of old 'China hands' and companies, had their monies with the 'Honkers and Shankers', the Hong Kong and Shanghai Banking Corporation – better known in the UK as HSBC. All took steps to cover their downside risk. The perceived effect of the handover was felt at all levels of Hong Kong society. One of the most poignant conversations,

I heard in the bar of the Hyatt Hotel, Kowloonside. The two elderly Englishmen sat at the bar were the prime example of the retired Colonial. Formal attire: collar and tie, and crested blazer, despite the humidity outside. I seem to recall the SAS being mentioned.

"Well. I suppose there's nothing else for it," said the one, gloomily. "If the Chinese are moving in, then we'll have to move out – back to Blighty."

"Mmm, suppose we will," said the other, equally despondent. "Still, look on the bright side: the damp climate and the first English winter will probably see us off…"

I never saw them again, but I'd like to think they survived the change in climate. Also leaving, for different reasons, were the Triads. Only too aware of the Chinese punishment handed out to organised criminal gangs – namely execution – they moved the majority of their operations to Los Angeles, New York and London.

I sometimes wish I could move the Hong Kong transport infrastructure to England: it works. Hong Kong's MTR System comprises ten lines and the Airport Express, also the Light

Railway to the New Territories and the Chinese border. On Hong Kong island, the blue double-decker buses and red double-decker trams are a reminder of 150 years of British rule.

The ferries offer regular services to Kowloon, the outlying islands and over to Macau – once a Portuguese colony and gambling Mecca – and to mainland China. The Peak Tram is the steepest funicular railway in the world, from Garden Road up 1200 feet to the summit, with a panoramic view from the Peak Tower Sky Terrace over Hong Kong's skyline, or, from Lugard Road Lookout, over Victoria Harbour to Kowloon.

The Peak has always been the measure of social status in Hong Kong. The higher up the Peak, the more important the person. I was on the Peak, but only just – I was nearer the bottom of the social ladder than the top. One insight into the Colonial pre-occupation of social status is, that from 1888, the tram was for the exclusive use of the British Governor and residents of the Peak. I am not too sure what their opinion would be of Madame Tussaud's in the Peak Tower Complex or Disneyland on Lantau Island.

The Star Ferry across Victoria Harbour from Kowloon to Hong Kong island is an experience. As a new arrival, I had asked why the upper deck was more expensive than the lower. I got a very logical, Chinese answer:

"Lower deck sink first."

Waiting for the ferry at the down ramp gate are a heaving mass of local Cantonese. Orderly queueing is not a Chinese habit. I was wondering why the Chinese attendant was sizing up the crowd with a look of abject terror. Then I found out. Suddenly, he jumped onto the barred gate as it swung open and clung on for his life. Had he fallen, he would have been trampled underfoot. I have witnessed several stampedes, animal and human, on several continents, but never one as totally unnerving as the Chinese variety.

One of the first pieces of advice I was given on arrival was:

"If you fall in the harbour, rush straight to hospital – the kids swimming in it have an inbuilt immunity – in your case get a jab for every disease known to man."

Luckily, I never had to follow his advice. However, reading the menu in the restaurant of the Hyatt Hotel in Kowloon, there was a starter of 'Crap Soup'. I knew it was obviously a misprint. Well, it was probably a misprint. Was the chef trying to warn the customers? In any event, I chickened out and ordered a Caesar Salad. Going native, I took a sampan from the Typhoon Shelter, a floating community, the sampans selling food are the ultimate in home delivery, more boat-to-boat than door-to-door.

Of the expensive floating restaurants of Aberdeen Harbour, I critiqued the 'Jumbo' – its interior replicating an Imperial Palace – which can hold 2,300 diners at one sitting. The critique: a gourmand's idea of six-star heaven.

The Man Mo Temple I still find an enigma. Named after Man, the god of literature, and Mo, the god of war, the only logical conclusion is that it must make a difference to the Chinese if they're slaughtered by someone who's well-read.

One has to appreciate that gambling is not a pastime to the Chinese – it is a way of life. My Cantonese friends would bet a fortune on two cockroaches crawling up a wall. Built on reclaimed marshland in 1846, Happy Valley

Racecourse is a Hong Kong institution. The season, determined by climate, is from September to early July, with night racing the most popular. I learned to give it a wide berth while I still had a shirt.

For some serious shopping, I headed for Kowloonside and Cheung Sha Wan Road – fashion street – for the latest designer fashions at wholesale prices thanks to over-runs and rejects. The Fleamarket is good for electronics at bargain prices, but I prefer the night market on Temple Street, after sunset. This market has literally everything, even fortune-tellers – the Chinese really are superstitious.

It was in Temple Street I picked up my Pierre Cardin suit, which I wore to my (second) wedding. I did not advertise the fact it had cost me the equivalent of ten new pence. I still have it.

It was in a Kowloon bar that I learned to stop a fight before it starts. It is never a good idea to get into a fight in Hong Kong – watch the locals practicing their martial arts *kata* in the parks in the early morning. I used to join them. I have been practicing the *budo* – martial arts – since the age of ten. I never fight.

I was simply enjoying a cold *Tsing Tao* while people watching. More specifically, I was watching a group of young, perfectly harmless, Japanese tourists, and, at the table next to them, a group of equally young, but very loud – and very drunk – Australians. One of them, encouraged by his mates, lifted his right leg and deposited it on the lap of the nearest Japanese youth. Every time the Japanese tourist removed the offending leg, back it came onto his lap. I knew some Japanese from my time there, enough to work out what was going to happen next in retaliation for the Australian's insult.

At this juncture, I decided to do the not-so-smart thing and intervene. I approached the Australian's table with my best Aussie accent (Yes, I've lived there too).

"G'day – is there a prob'?"

They confirmed there was, if it involved Japanese. I nodded in the direction of the Japanese' table.

"if you look at his right hand, you'll see his centre knuckle's extended, it's called a phoenix fist." I lowered my voice. "Whatever that hits it's going through and out the other side. See how his mates are tensed. They're getting ready to do you some really serious damage. I'd say this would be an ideal time for damage limitation, wouldn't you?"

They took my advice, and left. The Japanese table smiled, bowed and bought me a *Kirin*.

★ ★ ★ ★

Taiwan, the Republic of China, lies between the East and South China Seas; southwest of Okinawa, north of the Philippines and off the southeast coast of the Peoples Republic of China – and therein lies the problem. The ROC and the PRC can prove a diplomatic minefield if planning to visit both. I had no choice, I had a feature to write. For decades there were no direct flights to Taiwan from China; it was possible only by going to the ROC office in Hong Kong for a visa and flying to Taiwan on China Air. There were no direct flights from China until 2008.

The root cause of the problem is simple: the PRC would like the ROC returned to them, as they consider it part of the Middle Kingdom.

Taiwan, the Republic of China, came into being as a result of the Chinese Civil War. It is the oldest surviving republic in East Asia. In 1911, the new ROC replaced the two-thousand-year-old rule of the Quing Dynasty. So, although the Republic was established on mainland China in 1912, when the Kuomintang lost the civil war to the Communists in 1949, Chiang Kai – Shek evacuated the government from Nanking to the island of Formosa (Taiwan) with Taipei as its provincial capital.

He also took the whole of China's gold reserve with him.

The Communists were, understandably, more than a little miffed.

Their avowed intention remains to take Taiwan by military force should diplomacy fail. The military installations on Taiwan's Fujian coast are a result of the threat of invasion. Their first – if not only – defence, is to hold out until the USA can come to their assistance. Intelligence would seem to suggest that the PRC may well wait until the USA is busy elsewhere before making a military move, or consider the USA would not want a Third World War triggered by Taiwan.

Ironically, despite being founder members of the United Nations and one of the first five nations comprising the UN Security Council, in 1971 the ROC was replaced in the UN by the Peoples Republic of China. One can only come to the conclusion that the UN had an eye on its future.

At one time, I was a regular passenger from Hong Kong to Taipei with China Air. I never flew First Class. This was entirely the fault of Billy Connelly, who pointed out 'planes very seldom back into a mountain'. I console myself with that thought when I find myself flying into a typhoon in the South China Sea.

With a population of over 23 million, Taiwan's capital on its northern tip, accounts for over 2 million. Interestingly, although 85% of the population are descended from mainland Chinese, 49% consider themselves Taiwanese, and only 3% Chinese; 44% consider themselves both. Whichever group they belong to, they are as superstitious as their mainland neighbours. I was once severely admonished by my floor concierge in Taipei for whistling one evening. Evidently, whistling is an invitation to ghosts to show themselves.

The quickest way I know to alienate oneself in Taiwan is to have too much to drink. This is considered immature, and indicative of a lack of self-confidence. I never realised how immature I was until I tried the local 140% proof *kaolang,* the distilled grain liquor. I not only lost face, I also lost my wallet.

The Taiwanese calendar system I also found confusing. In fact, two calendars are used: The Gregorian (no problem), and the Minguo, which numbers the years from 1912 (problem). This means expiry dates can be eleven years out. To further complicate matters, the Lunar Calendar is used for festivals such as Chinese New Year and the Dragon Boat Festival.

Taiwan is an island of contrasts: the Central Mountains and coastal area with its scenic Sun Moon Lake, and, the east, cut off from the rest of the island by its mountains, and home of the incredible beauty of the Taroko Gorge, rightly the premier attraction of Taiwan. Still home to the Formosan Black Bear and wild boar, the gorge rises to 12,200 feet. The gorge's original inhabitants were the Atayal – face-tattooing head-hunters, with similarities to the natives of the South Pacific. To say one has 'done' the gorge, it is obligatory to have hiked its length, following the Liwu River. The Baiyang Waterfall and Golden Canyon provided me with the best photo opportunities, as did the suspension bridge to the Hasiangte Temple, on a cliff overlooking the valley.

My base, the teeming city of Taipei, which boasts over 30,000 street vendors, is home to the National Palace Museum and the Longshan Temple. Language: Mandarin; religions: Buddhism and Taoism; Transport: horrendous. Driving on the right I can cope with, but not in one of the most densely populated places on the planet. The sheer volume of cars, taxis, motorcycles, scooters and bicycles – and an utter disregard for any semblance of traffic rules or right of way – ensures driving is not an option. There are traffic lights, but, as near as I could ascertain, red means 'Go', amber: accelerate, and green: go like a bat out of hell and turn in front of oncoming traffic. I suppose this can be expected in a country where you can be issued with a driving licence without ever having seen a road. Take a taxi. On second thoughts – don't. The worst traffic offenders and danger to life and limb *are* the taxi drivers. There is no safety in being a passenger rather than a pedestrian.

As my cab pulled up outside my Taipei hotel, I noticed the hotel doorman, who had already written down my destination, was now noting down the taxi's registration. I asked why.

"Is only precaution – our prisons are full. Drivers are on parole – they give them jobs as taxi-drivers."

I just had to ask.

"Notes are for your protection. We call your destination to make sure you arrive."

"And if I don't?"

"Then I call police," he smiled.

That made me feel a whole lot better...

On my last trip, I was not so lucky in my choice of hotel. The problems began as my porter showed me to my room. Having tipped, I closed the door. The entire lock fell off. I called reception.

The hotel handyman spent twenty minutes replacing the lock. I tipped for the second time. I closed the door. The lock fell off. I changed rooms.

That evening, I was invited for drinks with a fellow Englishman, in Taipei on business. He insisted we go to Taipei's only real English pub, run by an English divorcee. I asked her what major running costs were in Taiwan.

"Bribery, corruption and protection."

We stayed longer than intended, and I did not get back to my hotel until the early hours. I took the elevator to my floor with only one thing on my mind: sleep. My floor concierge had other plans.

"You like company, yes?"

"I like company, no."

"You like beautiful girl – University student? Very clean. I bring four – you choose, yes?"

"No!"

"Okay, you like beautiful boy – University student? Very clean I bring four – you choose, yes?"

This was becoming more than a little tiresome.

"For the last time, *No!* I need to sleep."

"Okay – I know," he tapped the side of his nose with his finger. You like something different, yes?"

I'd no idea what he had in mind. I did not want to know…

By now, he was starting to turn aggressive. He grabbed my lapels with both hands. I am usually noted for my patience. This wasn't one of those times. I clamped a nerve hold on his right wrist, holding his arm straight out as I kicked him under his right armpit. I went to bed. Next morning, as I mentioned this to the management to cover my own downside risk, I was apologetically informed that he had a broken shoulder, and had been dismissed.

If you're in the market for a wristwatch, Taipei is the place to be. With a reputation for electronics and manufacturing, Taiwan is also a major player in fake designer goods – including watches. My friend of the evening before, had just bought several.

"I give them as Christmas presents," he had explained, smiling. "I would love to see their faces when they realise they bought me a book token, and their present is a Rolex Oyster. Here's the number," he had handed me a card, "give them a call and they'll bring a case full of samples to your hotel room."

I did, and became the proud owner of a Rolex Oyster Day-Date. At least, I was, until I took it to a London jeweller's for a new Rolex metal strap (real), which would cost substantially more than I paid for the watch. How was I to know all jewellers were under a legal obligation to confiscate any fake watches brought in for repair.

★ ★ ★ ★

My next trip, from Taiwan to Manila for a meeting with Philippine Airlines, coincided with the birthday celebrations of President Ferdinand Marcos at the Manalapan Palace. The Republic of the Philippines lies directly south of Taiwan, only a few hundred miles from Borneo to the south-west, and is the third largest English-speaking country in the world. Due to its colonisation by Spain from the 1520s, it is not surprizing that 83% of the 90 million plus population are Roman Catholic. Less well-known is that, upon its independence in 1898, the Philippines became the first, and only, regional colony of the USA. A classic melting pot of Malay, Chinese, American, Spanish and Arabs, eleven million Filipinos work overseas. The Americans seem to mainly employ them as domestics, while Englishmen, given the number of internet dating and marriage sites, see Filipino girls as potentially younger brides.

With a tropical climate averaging 80°F, I avoid visiting in the high- humidity hot season of April and May. As the rainy season – including the Monsoon Season – lasts from June to November, where possible, I try to arrange a Philippines visit in the coolest season of December to February, ideal for a Christmas or New Year break. Ignore the fact that the islands have active volcanoes and are in the West Pacific Typhoon Belt, and on the Pacific Rim of Fire – I do.

Although Quezon City is larger, the capital of Manila is on the northern island of Luzon. I use the word 'capital' loosely, it is really a collection of towns, with no city centre as such, and manic. When I was last there, the transport system – with a very small t – was 'interesting'. The bus system was a classic: no timetables and no bus station. It was the only destination I knew of where you had to take a taxi to find a bus.

Taxis, or the colourful jeepnies, prove that Manila is a serious contender with Taipei for the title 'Worst Drivers on the Planet'. A rental car is not an option given the traffic jams and extortionately expensive tollways.

You could take the train – if you could find one. The Philippines National Railway was obviously named by someone with delusions of grandeur. It had only one line, from Manila to the south-west – but only if they could find enough antique rolling stock to make up a train on the day. If a timetable existed – which it doesn't – it could be printed on a postage stamp.

Manila's hotels compare favourably with any other capital city, however, many cater specifically for Japanese tourists, so a Japanese phrase book may be more useful than Spanish. My hotel was always an easy choice: The Manila Hotel at Rizal Park, a throwback to the days of Colonialism from its pill-box hatted bellboys to its genteel air of faded decadence. The hotel - once owned by Marcos – has earned its accolade as one of Asia's grand hotels. During my time there, the General Manager was Franz, whose claim to fame was his swim through shark-infested waters to escape the Japanese. Ironically, a great number of the hotel's guests are now Japanese. Franz had put me in the Macarthur Suite, from the balcony of which the General had given his famous 'I shall return' speech.

Manila is a vibrant city, pulsating with nervous energy and with a frisson of dangerous excitement by night. Makati, Manila's business centre by day, becomes the hub of the city's nightlife. There are too many nightclubs than are good for the liver. The Casino-Filipino is government-controlled legal gambling, from roulette to poker – and even Bingo for the English. As it is near the airport, it's possible to kill time before your flight and return home stony broke.

On the morning of President Marcos's birthday, I had a meeting scheduled with Philippine Airlines in Makati. That the airline had been given to Imelda Marcos as a birthday present from her husband, I presumed, of course, was only a rumour. Franz advised me it would be quicker to walk through Rizal Park in order to pick up a cab. The park was thronged with dancing crowds, celebrating their

President's birthday with their congratulatory banners and music.

At the far side of Rizal Park, I hailed a cab to the high-rise headquarters of Philippine Airlines. I should have known better, but I got into the taxi without checking the meter. When we drew up at my destination, the driver demanded his fare. This was slightly less than for an all-day tour of Manila. He made it clear I was not leaving the cab until the fare was paid, plus tip.

"I am a guest of your government," I pointed to the two, armed security guards at the entrance to the building. "Shall we ask them to sort out this problem?"

The driver leaned over and opened my door with a look of abject fear.

"No, please! No fare! Please, no fare!"

Another wonderful commendation for Marcos's forces of law and order. Suffice it to say, I was not sorry to see the overthrow of the Marcos regime.

Chapter Nine
From a Toilet in Turkey

I should have known when my arrival in Turkey got off to a bad start, I was going to need the dedicated Nurse this trip. The transfer from Dalaman Airport to the hotel, should have been straightforward. Unfortunately, our driver had no idea where our hotel was located in Olüdeniz – in fact he had difficulty in locating Olüdeniz. Once he'd found the town, he had to admit he was totally lost. We then spent over an hour looking for our hotel. I had him stop, while I asked a group of passing tourists for directions. We eventually arrived at the hotel after a total transfer time of what felt like a fortnight.

I did not tip.

It was now 4.00am. The hotel reception was deserted. Then I noticed the pile of blankets on a settee. They were moving. I gently pulled back the blankets and rugs to reveal the receptionist, aged about fifteen. He grabbed a bunch of keys off the wall and led us, dragging our baggage, to a flight of steps leading down to an underground bunker which had never seen natural light.

I had researched the hotel in detail before leaving the UK. It was just as well. I had found it was hotel policy to put late arrivals into the dungeon for 'the first night only'. They then informed the incarcerated guests the next day, that the hotel was full and that they had no other rooms available. I presumed this was the only way they could fill the room.

As a travel writer, I travel anonymously, but, in this situation, I had little choice but to produce my business card and press ID. His English suddenly improved, and he ran back to reception. Upon his return, he informed us there was one other room available he had overlooked, a garden room with a patio.

We slept for thirteen hours.

Olüdeniz, on Turkey's south-west Turquoise Coast, is justifiably famous for its Blue Lagoon National Park, a UNESCO World Heritage Site. Once we had liberated a table and two chairs from the pool area and transferred then to our patio, we spent what little of the day was left on the quieter landside of the lagoon to relax. A full itinerary lay ahead.

We took the *Dolmus,* the local bus, to Hisarönü, connecting to Kayakoy to investigate why this village had been abandoned, and known as 'Peace City'. The earliest recorded city in the Kaya Valley had been Karmillos, a classic Lycian city. At its height, it had consisted of 500 houses, 2 large and 4 small churches, 20 chapels, 2 schools and its own local newspaper, serving its 2,500 inhabitants.

As usual, 'the Nurse' climbed up the mountainside for a photo shoot. I needed to find out why it had been deserted. The answer, which I had found in similar situations, was religion. In 1923, at the end of the Turkish War of Independence, based on religious justification, it had been agreed to an exchange of Turkish and Greek populations. In the months that followed, many of the Greek inhabitants were less than happy at their compulsory resettlement. They returned to Macedonia. There followed a compulsory eviction of all Greeks. Now a protected historical site, Kayakoy remains a 'ghost town'.

A personalized government tour to the Taurus Mountains had been arranged, with official government guide: Oz', a sweet and knowledgeable girl, and car. The first destination was Tylos, city of the Hittites, Alexander the Great, and the Roman, Byzantine and Ottoman Empires. My primary interest was the excavation of the agora, baths and a hippodrome seating 5,000 spectators. The climb up the steep walls of the Acropolis, I sensibly delegated. In retrospect, I may have missed a 'must see': a 2nd century example of early recycling. The Romans discovered all the tombs, carved out of the rock, had sitting tenants. With typical Roman efficiency, they removed the incumbent bones and replaced them with the bodies of their own citizens, as they died.

We drove further into the mountains, to the Yaka Trout Farm, its several levels of pools fed by the melting snow from the mountain peaks. As to lunch, I doubt I shall ever dine on fresher trout – literally from pool to plate.

A 6.00am start for the long journey north to the ancient city of Ephesus, to the west of the great trade route through the Cayster Valley to Asia. The city was first recorded in the middle of the 7th century BC and under the protection of

Athens from 454BC until captured by Alexander the Great in 334BC. In 133BC the city came under Rome, who considered it the most important Province in the reign of Augustus.

St. Paul spent three years in Ephesus from 53AD, introducing Christianity. St. John the Apostle and the Virgin Mary – who had been placed under his care by Jesus – came to Ephesus between 37AD and 42AD. The Virgin Mary died in Ephesus in her 60s and was secretly buried by St. John to avoid her becoming a martyr and object of pilgrimage.

Ephesus' impressive, pillared Celcus Library was completed in 125AD, containing 12,000 book rolls, but was burned down by the Goths in 265AD. A foot, carved in the roadway, has the inscription 'Follow me', and leads to the city brothel. The city's public toilets seated 50 people at one time. Each citizen had a personal slave stood behind him, to wipe his posterior.

Near the 2nd century Odeum, seating 1500 spectators, and originally covered by a wooden roof, is the Temple of Artemis and the Basilica of St. John. A major site for Christian visitors is the House of the Virgin Mary, where she reputedly spent her last years. The Roman stone-built church, was erected over her house and grave in the 4th century AD.

After an overnight stay, on to Pamukkale and its thermal pools, with a calcium cascade creating snow-white terraces of 'cotton', as it has throughout its 1400-year history. It is possible to swim around ancient underwater columns in the Pool of Cleopatra.

Hieropolis, the Holy City, so called because of its many temples. The majority of the city is a Roman rebuild, following a series of earthquakes. The one-mile long main street, is a mixture of public buildings, shops and homes. The 2nd century AD Nymphaeum supplied water to the houses from the Monumental Fountain, in front of the Temple of Apollo. The octagonal Martyrium is in honour of St. Philip the Apostle who was said to have married in Hieropolis in 80AD. Either the date is wrong, or he was a very active 100-year old…

Next on my itinerary: The Necropolis, the City of the Dead, with graves from Hellenistic and Roman periods. As usual, these was segregated by class: a mixture of tumulus and sarcophagus for the wealthy, and box-shaped public and family graves for the poor. My particular interest was the amphitheatre, built in the reign the Emperor Hadrian in the 2nd Century AD.

Unfortunately, I was the only one who *was* interested. My mobility problems ruling out climbing up to it, the only option was one of the white, 'small coach' taxis. The driver said he wasn't interested in taking one passenger – it was not worth his while. I did see the amphitheatre, but it cost me the fare for five passengers…

I was congratulating myself on a comparatively travail-free day, when 'the Nurse' pointed out my right leg was infected and swelling fast, caused by a small cut. This is where travelling with a nurse becomes of paramount importance. Being disabled, I am often asked what I would recommend. Easy – marry a nurse. You will not get sympathy, but you will get a diagnosis and treatment.

Back in Olüdeniz, my infection was lanced, and my leg bandaged. The next morning, I could not walk. As 'the Nurse' returned from the pharmacy with antibiotics, probiotics and anti-inflammatories, I prescribed myself a bottle of Raki.

I asked myself, 'What else could go wrong?'

I added an acute chest infection to my list.

The following morning, with a change of bandages, I limped to the local bus, rattling with painkillers, to Koy and Gemila Beach, a quiet and secluded cove. From the beach, we bribed a local fisherman to take us across to St. Nicholas Island. As 'the Nurse' headed for the summit, to check-out the churches, I got the better end of the deal. The government-appointed Curator of the island, its only inhabitant, took pity on me. I spent the afternoon in his garden, as we ate delicious, freshly-picked cherries, washed down with copious pitchers of local red wine. By the time the boatman returned to pick us up, I was feeling no pain.

That evening in Olüdeniz, I fulfilled the part of my brief to select one restaurant from many, to recommend. On the way to the beach, one had to run the gauntlet of restaurant staff, touting for business. All of them promoted the 'full English breakfast'. One had gone a step further: on his chalk-board menu, he was promoting *'Real Tesco Sausages!'*

My choice of recommended restaurant was the Blue Star garden restaurant: their Anatolian lamb is to kill for, served by the white gloved waiters, with wine recommended by the atelier.

The following morning, my leg infection had spread. I diagnosed it as gangrene. 'The Nurse' disagreed. It was just in time for the most horrendous travail this trip.

★ ★ ★ ★

If you suffer from easily offended sensibilities, I'd suggest you skip what follows – Author.

We reached the village of Kabak in the coastal mountains by a series of hair-raising bends, but worthwhile for the panoramic views over the ravines to the inlets and coves by the sea. The only restaurant overlooking the coast was not yet open for the season, but managed to rustle up an omelette on request.

I wish they hadn't.

I relaxed on the upstairs sundeck, as the Nurse clambered down the ravine for a photo shoot. After an hour, she returned and joined me at the table. As she did, with a loud trumpet, I literally exploded. This was not your common or garden 'Turkish Trots' – this was more akin to a major volcanic eruption. 'The Nurse' leapt into action. She pulled my, now brown, shorts down around my ankles, and began a mop-up operation with bottled mineral water and paper serviettes. In the middle of the mop-up, the waitress appeared at the top of the stairs, folded her arms, and, smiling, became an avid spectator. I could only conclude she was not the sharpest knife in the box. Needless to say, I hurriedly pulled up my shorts, left the money for lunch on the table, and took the stairs down from sundeck, with the accompaniment of what could only be described as loud squelching sounds.

Back on the road, we saw a disused, ramshackle wooden outside toilet – a godsend. Or so we thought. We retreated inside the toilet, with no glass in the windows, and continued the mopping up operation, using water from the non-flushing cistern. Eventually, Operation Mop-up completed, we found we couldn't get out. The toilet door had securely locked itself. We were trapped in an abandoned outside toilet on top of a mountain in Turkey.

Things could only get better.

After urging each other not to panic, we panicked. We began shouting "Help!" in several languages. After what seemed a fortnight, an old, shawled lady in her eighties, and bent double, hobbled towards us.

She stood, shaking her head in disapproval. She had come to the obvious – and wrong – conclusion as to why we would want to be in the toilet together. Tutting her disapproval, she hobbled off, oblivious to our pleas.

Some twenty minutes passed.

Suddenly, the old lady hobbled back and frowned at us in silence. Finally, she produced not a key, but a metal clamp-like contraption. Several minutes later, the door swung open to a chorus of "Thank you" in Turkish. I wrapped a beach towel around my nether regions, knotted at the waist. I didn't have much choice, having buried my shorts. We hid until the local bus arrived.

What an 'interesting' day.

At the end of the week, somehow, both my legs had swollen to twice their normal size. I left Turkey with both legs bandaged from ankle to crotch. I arrived back in England in a wheelchair. I am afraid, for me, this is not necessarily unusual.

★ ★ ★ ★

The Gambia. Brief: the feasibility of extending the tourist season, based on infrastructure rather than climate only. Surrounded by Senegal on three sides, Gambia's west coast at the mouth of the River Gambia, had been its only direct access historically. In the late 17th and early 18th centuries, Britain and France fought over possession until the 1783 Peace of Paris Agreement ceded Gambia to the British as a Crown Colony. Although English is the official language, in reality, the majority of the population speak Mandinka.

The etiquette of mealtimes I initially found somewhat complicated. Family and friends sit on a *basing* - a mat – with a large food bowl in front of them, usually containing a mound of rice in the centre, topped with a sauce. You must only eat from the section in front of you with the fingers of your right hand – the left, being used in the toilet, is considered an insult.

In Gambia, following the greeting of *"Naka naga def"* and the response of *"Mang fi rekk"*, it is polite – but a mistake – to enquire about the health of their family. This can result in a thirty minute or more conversation.

In the 300 years of a flourishing Atlantic slave trade, it is estimated that some 3 million slaves had been taken by the slave-catchers, some sold by their village, and some from hostile villages after a raid. The majority had been sold to the European market as servants, a status symbol among the aristocracy and wealthy families until, suddenly, there became a huge market in the plantations of the West Indies as cheap labour.

Although Britain abolished the slave trade throughout its empire in 1807, this met with little success in the Gambia, where it continued until 1906. With a population of under two million, Gambia under President Jammeh proved 'interesting'. The President claimed he could cure AIDS with bananas, and that homosexuals were 'vermin', and should be dealt with as malaria-carrying mosquitos. One could say, the government's policies did not include civil liberties and freedom of the press. One could – I didn't. I did not go out of my way to be critical in public. Declaring the Commonwealth a 'neo-colonial institution', the President ended Gambia's membership and, in 2015, declared the country an Islamic Republic.

Tourism is by far the greater part of Gambia's economy, hence my brief, which I found increasingly turning into investigative journalism.

Wherever you walk in Gambia, you will find yourself running the gauntlet of children of all ages. I have a theory, somewhat unkindly, that the children are taught not 'Mamma' as their first word, but 'dollar'. I was approached by teenagers with clipboards every time I ventured outside the hotel, and asked to sponsor their football team. I calculated there must have been more youth football teams in one town than the total number of football teams in Europe.

On sponsorship, be prepared for your hotel staff to approach you asking if you will sponsor them for a UK visa to enable them to work there and send money back to their families. I talked to an inundated British Consulate: understandably, for a UK visa, in addition to a sponsor, applicants must have an offer of employment in the UK, and/or a return flight ticket and proof of family and finances in Gambia to guarantee their return, for a temporary visa.

On with my fact-finding tour: recommend places to visit.

The Bao Bolong Wetland Reserve, on the north bank of the Gambia River, consists of mangrove forests, salt marshes and savannah, ensuring a bird watchers paradise, with over 540 species of birds, including herons, storks, egrets, sandpipers, kingfishers and Senegal parrots. For those who prefer their wildlife wild, there are crocodiles, hyena, and antelope. The River Island National Park is noted for its native baboons.

The Abuko Nature Reserve contains the Chanchikally Crocodile Pool. The braver tourists can stroke a heavily sedated crocodile, before being relieved of a fee (in US$ rather than Gambian Dilasi) to feed the crocodiles. None of them looked as if they were exactly starving to death on my visit.

For shoppers, the bustling, colourful Prince Albert Market in Banjul, named after Queen Victoria's Consort, is worth a visit. The hundreds of rickety street stalls offer fabrics, woodcarvings, crafts and street-food. As ever, bargain down the prices.

Tourists are encouraged to visit Arch 22. Not by me.

Built to commemorate the 1994 military coup which overthrew the democratically elected government, it looks rather like a slope-rooved house on a platform of pillars, 125 feet high, on three floors. The second floor is a gallery, offering panoramic views of Banjul. The day of my visit, the President of Mali was expected on a state visit. Schoolchildren, from primary school age, had been bussed in, given Mali national flags, and shepherded into orderly lines, those wearing school uniforms placed at the front.

The children were understandably impatient with anticipation, pushing forwards, hoping for a glimpse of the visiting President. The uniformed police and security did not share my idea of crowd control. They laid into the children, left and right, with their version of the *lathi* – the long wooden pole commonly used as a club by the police in India. Any child breaking the line was subjected to the club.

The security police attempted to confiscate my camera. Unsuccessfully - I still have the photos.

★ ★ ★ ★

Onto, in my humble opinion, the most blatant scam in Gambia.

A river cruise will take the tourist on what is now known as 'The Kunta Kinteh Cruise', to Juffureh Village, where the central character of Alex Haley's *'Roots'*, had allegedly been born. The first port of call was St. James Island, with its ruined British fort, which had been unsuccessful in stopping the slave trade. The island has a small primary school, a slavery museum with a few chains and manacles and a large thatched roundhouse for music recitals.

Stepping ashore at the small jetty, the first thing that greeted me was a table straining under the weight of its combination of exercise books, felt tips, ink pens, pencils and all things considered necessary for a primary school – and all substantially over their recommended retail price. Outside the single storey school, the pupils were assembled in an orderly group, to sing for the tourists. As the singing began, the tourists lined up to place their recently-purchased gifts on a large trestle table: 'US dollars also welcome'. Calculating the number of tourists visiting the island each day, the school must, by now, have a massive surfeit of educational materials.

Lest you think me a cynic, on this trip I contributed a year's college fees for the education of the younger brother of my guide. Back in the UK, I received a letter from the principal of the College, asking me to pay for an entire new toilet block, in return it would be named after me. That, would have been a first.

The villagers wore traditional Gambian dress, posing outside their homes; several were seated, pounding away at a huge communal pestle and mortar. As soon as the tourists started to take photos, the trouble began. The village women suddenly demanded; "Dollars! Dollars!" One unfortunate lady had to be rescued by the tour guide. He advised her the only solution was to give them US dollars. I never would have guessed...

The recital of traditional Mandinka folk songs was held in the large, thatched roundhouse, played on the *kora* – rather like an oversize lute –

and a *djembe* drum. As we were leaving, I found my way blocked by the *kora* player'

"Salaam Aelikum!"

He ignored my greeting.

"Dollars! I want dollars!" he glared at me.

I replied to the threat with a "tsk, tsk," snapping my index finger and thumb together in rapid succession. In Mandinka, this indicates your displeasure. It had no effect.

"I need *mano* and *mburu!*"

I was sure he did need rice and bread, but he had already collected enough dollars for at least a month's shopping. He stepped towards me, threateningly, his English suddenly improving.

"I do this for a living – I want a tip!"

The gold top of my walking cane unscrews.

I gave him a tip: "Cut the aggression and you might do better."

At the same time, I turned the gold top of my cane one full turn to the right. He stepped back, drawing the obvious but erroneous conclusion, and, turning, stamped off.

The 'swordstick strategy' has got me out of trouble several times, in several countries.

And now: the highlight of the tour – being introduced to the actual descendants of Kunta Kinteh – the hero of Alex Haley's book and TV Miniseries. Everyone crowded into the Kinteh family's large thatched roundhouse, standing room only. The family, running the range of ages, were gathered around a bent, wrinkled and wizened central figure in a wicker chair: great grandmother, the head of the family.

In traditional costume, her head was swathed in scarves, leaving only her face visible. I estimated the year of her birth as around the time of Christopher Columbus. On her lap sat a huge wooden bowl, in anticipation of incoming dollars.

The 'audience' began with her great-grandsons, and several grandsons, lecturing on their family history, with numerous photographs being held up as 'evidence'. It was rather like listening to a synopsis of *Roots*. At the end of the talk, the audience were exhorted to give as much money as possible 'to help the poor'. The reward was a kiss from great-grandmother. That was me out. Dropping some dollars in the bowl, I skipped the kiss.

The average tourist was unlikely to pay a return visit. I paid a return visit. This time, the script was the same, but the cast was different – a completely interchangeable family. This time, I did not drop any dollars into the waiting bowl. This time, great-grandmother was even older than the previous one. I leaned forward as she pursed her lips, and whispered in her ear.

"Skip the anti-ageing cream – I don't think it's working."

On my way back to the jetty, I calculated the number of passengers/audience on each boat times the number of boats per day times the average donation of dollars. My conclusion: I was in the wrong business.

★ ★ ★ ★

For any reader who may think I am being a little unfair to Roots and Alex Haley, read on.

In 1976, Alex Haley's book and TV miniseries had become immensely successful. It purported to trace the history of his family through several generations. Haley was showered with awards, including the Prime Time Emmy Award for Outstanding Miniseries, the Golden Globe Award for Best Television Series – Drama; the George Foster Peabody Award for Distinguished and Meritorious Public Service (By Media), and, in 1975, a special Pulitzer Prize. He was also awarded several Honorary Doctorates. The series resulted in a hugely increased interest in genealogy, particularly among Afro-Americans searching for an identity.

Unfortunately for Haley, back in the USA, he was charged with plagiarism. Following a five-week Federal Court trial, Haley admitted in a statement that he 'acknowledged and regretted the various materials from *The African* by Harold Courtlander found their way into his book *Roots*. Having been proven to have read *The African,* Haley was found to have copied *81* passages into his book.

"*Roots*, takes from *The African,* phrases, situations, ideas and aspects of style and plot. The evidence of copying is clear and irrefutable."

– *Michael Wood, Professor of English, Columbia University and expert witness.*

Haley was accused by Federal Judge Ward that he had "perpetrated a hoax on the public." Haley was stripped of several of his awards and honorary doctorates. To date, Haley's book remains a notable exclusion from *The Anthology of Afro-American Literature.*

In February, 2009, *The Telegraph* reported "DNA proves Alex Haley has Scottish roots. The tests have established that Haley is clearly descended from a Scottish paternal bloodline."

Nevertheless, Kunta Kinteh Island remains as popular a tour as ever.

'You can fool some of the people all of the time'.

Chapter Ten
Berlin in Flames

C hristmas in Berlin, staying on the Kurfürstendamm – the Ku'damm to Berliners. Although now mainly designer shops, the two-mile long, tree-lined boulevard was once the crowded centre of the café society of the Prussian aristocracy.

Continuous heavy snowfall made no difference to Berlin's transportation network. In fact, extra services were scheduled for the holiday period. Unlike the UK, Berlin does not shut down for Christmas.

The Christmas markets have a unique and special atmosphere, their myriad wooden cabins and stalls offering everything from woodcarvings and hand-painted nativity sets, to smoked meat and cheeses, and fur hats and muffs. I grabbed a Thüringer würst – a hot dog German style and visited several glühwein stands to keep the circulation moving. At every stand, it's possible to buy and keep the decorated mug it is served in, the decoration being individual to each stand. I have a kitchen full. The German Christmas shops, offering everything you need for the festive season, are open every day of the year. Unfortunately, it never enters my mind to buy Christmas decorations in the middle of August.

Christmas Day, and the morning service at the new chapel in the ruins of the Kaiser-Wilhelm-Gedächtnis-Kirche, which had been destroyed by allied bombing in 1943. Being English, it was suggested to me I should look at the church's Cross of Nails. I did, and found it to be a gift from the people and Cathedral of Coventry, who had also suffered severe bomb damage. I found it sad that the only mutual tie lay in their destruction.

I had reserved a table for Christmas dinner at the Austeria on the Ku'damm, an old, traditional Berlin restaurant. We ordered the traditional German Christmas dinner: roast goose with potato dumplings, red and green cabbage (and copious red wine). I love goose, which used to be the traditional bird of choice for Christmas dinner for centuries in England, until turkey was introduced by the Americans. Over the next week or so, we met several of our Berliner friends for several lunches. The majority had decided to wait until meeting us for lunch before having their Christmas roast goose. The Nurse and I exchanged glances, but said nothing. I can honestly say that, upon our return to England, we were totally 'goosed'.

Having 'done' the Reichstag and the Tiergarten, we found ourselves at the Brandenburger Tor, originally a tollgate and conceived as an Arch of Peace, it had stood silent witness to the Nazi's 1933 torchlight procession to hail the beginning of a 1,000 Year Reich, and had later become an integral part of the infamous Berlin Wall.

My memories of Checkpoint Charlie are rooted in the Cold War. Then, it did not cater to the Russians and Americans with the now prolific franchises of McDonalds, Starbucks, Dunkin' Donuts, Burger King et al. Never revisit the past.

We decided to take a pleasant walk through a snow-covered Berlin down the Unter Den Linden. I forgot my propensity for accidents. Approaching the bridge to Alexander Platz, I walked over a patch of ice under its light dusting of snow. My legs shot forwards and upwards, and I fell heavily – and painfully – onto my back. With my track record, I should have known better than to think it was over. 'The Nurse' had been holding on to my arm. She fell on top of me. Unfortunately, her knee connected with my groin. It took ten minutes, and several Berliners, to haul me into anything resembling upright.

As Berlin is a multi-ethnic city, we headed for Kreutzberg, the Turkish Quarter. It did not take long to find the Tripping Stones – I tripped over one. They had been laid with the deliberate intention of attracting attention. I knelt, and cleared the snow from the simple, square brass plaque over which I had tripped. I translated its inscription: 'Here lies Paul Wolf. Deported 29.1.1943. Murdered in Auschwitz'. All the brass plaques set into the street have similar inscriptions. All were set outside the house from which the name on the plaque was taken.

My travails also seem to include immediate family.

It was meant to be a leisurely, relaxing lunch at the Lebensart on the Unter Den Linden. Here, I should explain, 'the Nurse' has a track record with candles.

The particular Christmas in question, we were renting a farm cottage. The nativity scene, the nurse had arranged on the hall window shelf, was complete with the stable with a straw floor and cotton wool snow around it, with a lit candle each side. Unfortunately, we were entertaining the cottage owner and his wife to dinner. The meal over, we moved to the sitting room for coffee. As we opened the connecting door, the room filled with dense, black smoke. The hall was not only filled with smoke – flames were licking at the ceiling. Problem: the hallway was our only way out. I began to mentally measure up the size of our coffee table to that of the plate glass window and, beyond, the garden.

I still have an aversion to being cremated before my time.

With the cost of a new hall window and shelf, complete redecoration and the results of smoke damage, it would have been cheaper to have spent Christmas abroad. I made it crystal clear that all use of cotton wool and candles as decoration for anything was now banned for life. At least, I thought, there would be no more fires at Christmas. Silly me.

We were perusing the menu when 'the Nurse' leaned over the candle in the centre of the table, to talk to her second son. I was alerted to the situation by second son, shouting "Mum!" Not exactly constructive. I looked up to see my wife's hair on fire. We are not saying singed here, or even glowing red, we are talking actual flames leaping up from her head.

"You're on fire!" caught her attention. I shouted to the staff:

"Hilfe! Mein Frau ist in flammen!"

Translation: "Help! My wife is on fire!"

This had no effect whatsoever, save eliciting giggles.

Grabbing the water jug, I emptied it over her head and threw a large table napkin over it. This proved more effective in attracting the staff's attention. They rushed her to the ladies toilet. Once they had put her out, one of the girls produced a headscarf to wear until we could find an emergency hair salon.

Being English, we then ordered lunch.

★ ★ ★ ★

It should have been straightforward: scheduled Air France flights via Paris, to Munich for the Christmas markets. As usual, the problems began before we could leave the UK.

"Okay guys – passports at the ready, please," as we approached departures passport control. I knew immediately when second son froze in paralysis, due, it transpired, to his passport still being in Cambridge. Following a damage limitation meeting, we took him down to the Easyjet desk, and booked him on a direct flight from Stansted, the next day. It was only later we pieced together the story of his journey.

He is registered with the National Autism Society, who issue sufferers of spectral autism with a special ID card confirming this, and requesting the holder be afforded every assistance. This was to become known in the family as 'playing the autism card'. The airport staff immediately implemented an assistance plan, escorting him to, and putting him on, the correct train for Cambridge.

What we did not know, was that he had arrived at Stansted – with passport – and 'played the card' for a second time. He was duly fast-tracked and escorted to the gate and allocated Priority Boarding. As a travel writer who spends half his life in airports, I am thinking of applying for a card myself. I am sure I can fake the symptoms.

Having checked into the Hotel Deutsches Theater, an excellent hotel in a less than salubrious Turkish area, next morning, we headed for the Christmas market in the Marienplatz, with its myriad stalls. Having stocked up on hand-carved wooden decorations, we concentrated on finding every *glühwein* stall in the market to avoid hypothermia at a temperature of 0°.

'The Nurse' went to the Frauenkirche Cathedral, at my request, to enable me to record her first impressions of the interior. Two heads are better than one. We found a table at the huge Augustiner Bräu Haus, brewers of the historic Augustiner beer, and really more of a beer hall than simply a restaurant, with an almost medieval atmosphere. Emulating the locals, we ordered the local weißwürst – white sausage – and beer.

The middle offspring arrived at our hotel at 9.00pm – having 'played the card' yet again. His mother pointed out he had missed the Christmas Market, which had closed late afternoon, and now only a distant memory. However, she also pointed out that he was still in time to accompany her to Christmas Eve Midnight Mass at the Cathedral. He did not look ecstatically overjoyed.

Christmas Eve tends to be the most important day in most of Europe, being the evening to exchange presents and the arrival of Santa Claus. Christmas day itself, is for visiting family and friends.

For Christmas dinner, I can recommend reputably Munich's best restaurant: The Ratskeller, under the Rathaus, the old Town Hall. I also recommended it for the disabled – it has a lift to the cellar restaurant. Dinner, obviously, was our traditional roast goose. Having toasted Christmas several times, we moved on to a pavement bar under the Cathedral, the Andechser am Dom, where I attempted to order a round of drinks.

"Drei weiß rot wein, bitte."

The waiter looked somewhat confused, shrugging his shoulders.

I tried again. Same reaction. I began to wonder if he understood his own language. The situation was now beginning to attract the attention of the other tables. It was then I suddenly realised what I was saying:

"Three white red wines, please."

No wonder he was confused. It was an impossible order – and acutely embarrassing for me.

I apologised and gave him the correct order. The other tables broke into a spontaneous round of applause. Not for the first time, I found myself looking for a crack in the cobbles.

The second offspring had booked himself on a day trip to Dachau. Not exactly a laugh a minute. I am pleased to report, the trip had a profound effect on him – the right effect. He cancelled his walking tour around 'Nazi Munich'.

I should have warned him, if travelling with me, you must expect at least one travail. He missed the tour, so caught a local train. It was the return journey which was to provide the problem. I should also have warned him to validate his train ticket in the machine, when he'd boarded the train. The return train had been boarded by two ticket inspectors. Checking his ticket, they had found it had not been validated. The inspectors had demanded an immediate €60 fine. He tried his best to explain he did not have enough cash. This, evidently, had an immediate reaction. Taking one arm each, they had frogmarched him to the nearest ATM. It refused to give him any money. They marched him to the next ATM, with the same result. Finally, several streets later, he found a friendly ATM and paid the fine. Dashing back to the station, he found he had missed his train.

Time to leave Munich. We went to the Air France desk to check-in. 'The Nurse' and I, no problem; second offspring, problem. As he had missed the first flight, his return flight had also been cancelled. The flight was full – no seats. Dash to the Easyjet desk. This was becoming a habit. He bought a ticket for a flight to Stansted, leaving at almost the same time as ours.

Checking, back in the UK, we found he had again 'played the card'. He had been fast-tracked at Stansted, and put on a train for Cambridge. To add insult to injury, he was home before us.

★ ★ ★ ★

Requiring two features, on the Bavarian and Austrian Alps, it made sense to combine the two, based in Bad Reichenhall in southern Bavaria. Bad Reichenhall was in the middle of a Venetian street festival when we arrived, with floats, bands, acrobats and fire-eaters, all in brightly coloured, historical costumes. We happily joined in the fun – especially in Ludwig's Bar with the locals, discussing politics – a good way to lose friends.

Dinner, we took at the Aegidi Cellar, dating back to 1159, and, with its subdued lighting and solid wooden furniture, rather like stepping back into a medieval inn.

The next day, I decided to take the double-decker Munich train to Freilassing, on the German-Austrian border, changing to a local train for the 'The City of Salt', Salzburg, and its Old Town. The Austrian piece was also to include cuisine, so, on arrival we headed straight for lunch at the well-known Zum Wilder Mann. You cannot reserve a table, but must find vacant seats at the wooden tables, joining the locals. It does not take long to make lifelong friends with the rest of the table, as the beer on tap flows freely, to accompany the famous Salzbürger Schnitzel.

After lunch, the funicular railway to the castle on the summit of the Monschberg Mountain, for a photo shoot of the panoramic views over a city seemingly covered in a light dusting of icing sugar.

We organized a second shoot from the imposing Hohensalzburg Fortress. From its ramparts, the two cities of Salzburg – the Old Town and the new town - become apparent, separated by the Salzach River.

Following my itinerary, we sauntered through the Old Town, covered with a fine blanket of snow, now turning to slush under the feet of the Christmas shopping crowds. From the Resident's Square, the Residenz itself being the 17th century Archbishop's Palace, to the Domplatz and Salzburg's Cathedral, a masterpiece of the Baroque style, with the impressive 1766 statue of the Virgin Mary in the centre of the Square

I should, perhaps, here confess that, in common with the majority of Salzburgers, I can't stand 'The Sound of Music'. Before I am burnt at the stake for heresy by its fanatical fans, who know the words to every song, I call a witness for my defence – Baroness Maria Augusta von Trapp. She lived in Vermont until her death in 1987. She several times made her views on the film known: she was not happy with the lack of accuracy in the story, nor the portrayal of the family. I remember one of her comments being, that, should they have escaped over the mountain shown in the film, they would have found themselves in an SS Barracks. I rest my case.

I should also admit that I love Mozart, not least because the cellar of the house in which he was born in 1756, is now a bar. Above, is a museum exhibiting his concert piano, clavichord, violins and viola. Joannus Chrysostomus Wolfgangus Mozart, turned his back on Salzburg in 1773, following a falling out with the Archbishop, his patron, and moved to Vienna. If you don't care for his music, but love chocolate, on the Getreidegasse is the shop of the original makers of Mozart Kugeln – universally known as 'Mozart's Balls'.

From Salzburg, we travelled by train to what seems to be a 'must visit' for tourists: Berchtesgaden, dominated by Germany's second highest mountain, The Watzmann. In the village, in 1934 Hitler bought a chalet known as the Berghof. It was destroyed by bombing in 1945, and the remains eradicated by the German Government in 1953 – and yet many tourists think they are there, whereas, if fact they are at the Eagle's Nest. This 'teahouse' had been built by Martin Bormann as a 50th birthday present for Hitler – a gift from the Nazi Party.

The visit got off to a disappointing start. The Eagle's Nest was inaccessible thanks to the heavy blizzards, in which we were caught. The only option was a visit to the Obersalzburg Documentation Exhibition. The purpose-built Centre is, in essence, a history of Hitler and the Nazi Party. In the tunnels and bunkers over which the Centre was built, visitors can pick up a wall-mounted telephone and listen to Hitler making one of his many speeches – a somewhat strange feeling. The exhibition itself provides a harrowing experience. I found one of the most horrifying exhibits was the range of illustrated and nauseatingly graphic anti-semitic books used to instil a hatred of Jews in primary schoolchildren. The memory stayed with me long after the trip.

The next day was my brother's 57th birthday, the reason we had invited him to join us as our guest on this trip. To celebrate, he tripped over the shower step and dislocated his shoulder. 'The Nurse' was not impressed, but disappeared, returning with bandages and a sling.

Nurses have no sympathy with their own families. As a hospital patient, I get a "Good morning – and how are you today?"; from my wife: "Oh, what's the matter with you *now*?"

Once bandaged and his arm in the sling, my brother was adamant we should stick to my itinerary. Consequently, we took the oldest gondola cable car in the world up the Predigtstuhl, Bad Reichenhall's highest mountain. Before taking the cable car, take out a second mortgage. From the cable car station, it is, in theory, safer to take the ice path, surrounded on both sides by walls of snow. Suddenly, as I looked to my left, I wondered if I was invisible. A skier, goggles down, was heading at speed straight for my head – with no intention of stopping.

"Down!"

We hit the deck. The skier jumped over the ice path, directly over our heads, and landed on the opposite side, disappearing down the off-piste slope, through the trees. I remember wishing I'd had a sniper's rifle. As we climbed above the Nebelungen layer, the summits of the other mountains appeared as islands in a sea of fog. Ever onwards and upwards, we eventually reached civilization, the Schlegelmulde, the only bar and restaurant on the summit, for hot soup and cold beer. Now above the fog and low cloud, the sky was a cloudless clear blue. With a blazing sun, it was necessary to discard layers of clothing. This was, in my experience, the only place I had found where one could get a sun tan and hypothermia all in the same day.

The following day, needing more material for my Salzburg piece, we again took the train to Freilassing, changing for the Salzburg train.

Once there, we made a beeline through the snow to the Marktplatz, and one of the city's institutions, its oldest coffee house: Tomaselli, dating from the 1700s. A major part of the experience is the staff. Traditional costumed waitresses wheel over a trolley, straining under the largest selection of gateaux, cakes and tarts in Salzburg. Having been served your selection, a waiter in black tie and white gloves, will approach your table. Examining your selection from the trolley, he will recommend a coffee to complement your choice. It never fails to give me the impression I have stepped back in time to the 19th Century café society of Vienna.

It was necessary to revisit the Hohensalzburg Fortress, dating from 1077, and one of the best-preserved in Europe. Looking from the battlements, below was only one house under the walls, isolated as an island in the middle of a snow-covered field. I went in search of the explanation. I found it. So strong were the feelings of the citizens of Salzburg that they refused to live anywhere near the castle's official executioner, so he was moved to this isolated house for the rest of, what must have been, a very lonely existence.

Heading for Salzburg's main railway station, I mused on what appeared to be a travail free day.

I must give up musing.

At the station's information office, I enquired if there was a direct train for Bad Reichenhall.

He assured me there was, in thirty minutes. I reiterated the question, and he assured me it was a direct train.

We settled into a carriage of the red and white local - but direct -train. In addition to 'the Nurse' and my brother, in our coach was also a shy and nervous eight-year old girl, whose mother had put her on the train in Salzburg with instructions that her aunt would meet the train in Bad Reichenhall.

When we reached Freilassing, on the border, 'the Nurse' pointed out an awful lot of passengers were leaving the train. I assured her this was a direct train, and we should remain where we were.

It was at precisely that second that the carriage was plunged into darkness. A second later, we heard the train's doors lock automatically. The little girl screamed. I lit my cigarette lighter to reassure her. (Yes, I come from the cigar-smoking generation, where the advertisements told us: '9 out of 10 doctors prefer Marlboro.'). Unfortunately, it lit up my face from beneath. Seeing this ghoul staring at her, she screamed even louder. My wife put an arm around her to calm her down, telling her she was perfectly safe, and that we would look after her.

Meanwhile, I was trying to prise open a window to attract attention, but to no avail. Trying to appear in control, I pronounced we would be found, as they could not leave the carriage here forever. The best course of action would be to sit down and remain calm. I didn't even sound convincing to me. I began to reconcile myself to spending all night in a railway carriage on the German – Austrian border.

After some fifteen minutes, the carriage's interconnecting door suddenly opened, and the train's driver stepped through. He looked more shocked than we were. Thank God he'd decided to do a final walk-through before heading off shift.

"What are you doing here?"

"Trying to get out!"

Stupid question.

"You are going to Bad Reichenhall?"

"It doesn't appear so."

"But you must change here!"

I made a mental note to kill the staff in the information office at Salzburg Station.

"Your train is there," he pointed to a train at the opposite platform. He looked at his watch. "It is leaving now."

"Well don't just stand there – stop it!"

He turned and disappeared. He reappeared running across the tracks to the Bad Reichenhall train.

He returned to tell us he'd held the train. Helping the little girl with her small suitcase, we took the underground subway to the other platform, and boarded the train.

At Bad Riechenhall, we stood with the girl. Almost immediately, a German lady in her forties, dressed for the weather, ran towards us, calling, we presumed, the girls name and sweeping her up into her fur coat. Eva, the little girl, told her all about her 'exciting journey'. Her aunt listened with pursed lips, then introduced herself, expressing her gratitude for ensuring her niece's safety. At that precise moment, a uniformed member of staff walked by. Unfortunately for him. She grabbed him, holding him by the lapels, and shouted at point blank range. He looked terrified. I didn't blame him. She went off like a five-megaton nuclear device in a small space. I decided it was not my responsibility to interfere. I didn't tell her I was the one who had said it was a direct train. She frightened the hell out of me too.

In any country where I understand and speak the language, I have one golden rule: don't. Well, at least, not for the first couple of days. Often, more can be gained by just listening.

An example was the coach transfer from Innsbruck Airport to a hotel in the Ziller Valley. I was in the front passenger seat, so was privy to the driver and his friend's conversation. He called the hotel which was our destination.

"Hi! We've got another bunch of English shithouses for you. ETA fifteen minutes."

I leaned forward. "Entschuldigung!" And, in German: "I have a favour to ask," I smiled. "I wondered if you could explain to me, please, what is the difference between an English shithouse and an Austrian asshole?"

They stopped smiling. The rest of the journey continued in silence.

Chapter Eleven
Tattoos and Transvestites

P *ōńnetia Tarani* – Oceana – The Society Islands – French Polynesia.

A seven-hour flight from Los Angeles, all over water: the Pacific Ocean. Looking down from a cloudless sky, the tall ships and schooners below appear as model's, floating upon a deep-blue, children's boating pond.

The Society Islands, comprised of the Windward and Leeward Islands, the Marquesas Islands and the Bass, Tuamotu and Gambier Islands were settled in 800 AD. The first European contact was not until 1521, when Ferdinand Magellan sighted Pukpuka in the Tuamotu Archipelago. Bora Bora was sighted by a Dutch explorer in 1722. Englishman Samuel Wallace visited Tahiti in 1767, followed by James Cook in 1769.

The London Missionary Society settled permanently in Polynesia in 1797. King Pomare was forced to flee to neighbouring Moorea in 1803, but was converted to the Protestant church, with all his people, in 1812. French missionaries arrived on Tahiti in 1834, but were expelled in 1836, which resulted in gunship diplomacy from France, who declared it a French Protectorate in 1842, its capital, Papeete, founded a year later. In 1880, France annexed Tahiti as a Colony, later claiming Tuamotu as part of its territory. Muraroa Atoll was used as an underground nuclear test site from 1974 – the last test was not until 1996. France declared Polynesia a French Collective in 2004.

French Polynesia is scattered over a little less than 1 million square miles of ocean. Of the total population, Tahiti accounts for around 70% of its 260,000, with 132,000 living in Papeete. Given the early arrival of the London Missionary Society, it is hardly surprizing that 54% of the population are Protestant. Unfortunately, visiting European sailors to the islands contributed prostitution, venereal disease, alcoholism, typhus, smallpox and influenza – decimating Tahiti's population. Today, the population is made up of 66.5% 'ethnically pure' Polynesian, with 11.9% European, predominantly French, the rest being of mixed race.

Tourism is the most significant part of the economy, but mainly to Bora Bora and Moorea. Tahiti, the largest island, contrary to film and television portrayals, has no natural sparkling-white, sand beaches. Being a volcanic island, its beaches are black sand, except where the resorts have paid large amounts to have a private beach created by dredging up and processing the white coral of the lagoons.

The Tahitian language is closely related to Rarotongan, Ma'áon and Hawaiian, although it is usually understood throughout the South Pacific Islands.

As usual, I carried the Tahitian language to extremes. 'The Nurse' and I arranged a Tahitian wedding, with traditional music and song, *leis* and orchids for the guests. The decision was not based on romance, but on the UK Registry Office not allowing any religious content to the ceremony. Consequently, once the English ceremony was over, we carried on and took our wedding vows in Tahitian, exchanging *leis* and shell (money) necklaces and, once officially married, moved our flowers from right to left ear; a flower behind the right ear means you are single and available, the left denotes taken. If married, try not to get the ears mixed up – that's known as divorce.

North-western Tahiti is *Tahiti Nui* or Big Tahiti; *Tahiti Iti* or *Taiarapu,* is the smaller, south-eastern part of the island. The interior is still virtually uninhabited. In Tahiti, I prefer to stay in an overwater bungalow, built on stilts with one side over the lagoon, with both a private sun deck and diving deck, enabling us easy access into the warm, turquoise bath that is the lagoon. It was as far as we needed to go to snorkel with the fishes and rays. Attracting them to our bungalow, we had down to a fine art: a morning routine of throwing pieces of our breakfast bread from our sun deck into the lagoon, morning and evening. After dark, the same result could be achieved by turning on the underwater lights.

As to why the South Sea Islands are a paradise for snorkelers and divers: the marine life can be described as being in eight groups. The first includes the popular Angel Fish, the Butterfly Fish, Damsel Fish and Moorish Idol. These multi-coloured lagoon fish swim in shoals of over fifty, enabling you to swim under your overwater bungalow surrounded by them. Group two are the Labrids and Wrasses, which are more active at dusk, and the Parrot Fish, with its beak-like jaws designed to feed off the coral. Porcupine Fish, Puffers, Trunk Fish and Trigger Fish make up the third group. Porcupine Fish and Puffers blow themselves up to twice their normal size as a defence against predators, while the Trunk Fish appears to be armour-plated, and the Trigger Fish has jaws like a steel trap.

Stone Fish, Leaf Fish and Scorpion Fish make up the group I have no wish to swim with. They all possess venomous spines on their fins, and can be fatal to snorkelers who disturb them. The laid-back, calm fifth group are Loachers and Groupers, the monarchs of the lagoon. Perches and Snappers make up the next category: they travel in large shoals for safety, as they are seen as lunch by sharks. Group seven are the Squirrel and Cardinal fishes, prolific but difficult to see as they are nocturnal and use caves and grottos as refuge. The final group includes Surgeon and Trumpet fishes.

Should you not see any of these groups when snorkelling, you are in the hotel pool.

To start the day, we took breakfast on our sun deck, compliments of the lagoon-side canoe delivery service. We found, when breakfasting on the sun deck, it was imperative to guard it with your life. We could not leave the table for a second. I did, to take a telephone call. By the time I'd returned, my breakfast had disappeared. The next morning, I discovered why: Mynah birds. Swooping down from the eaves of the straw roof, these mimics of the bird world made short work of anything edible. We found a solution which became a morning ritual. After feeding the fishes, we lay a line of pieces of fruit along the sun deck rail. From then on, they were happy to join us as we all ate breakfast together.

We took the local transport, *Le Truck,* into Papeete, like any other capital city, overcrowded. It is possibly worth the journey if you need a bank, boutique shopping or the indoor markets for traditionally woven palm baskets, fans, and *pareos* – the Tahitian sarong. I would not recommend trying the return journey by *Le Truck* – even if you can find the right queue – it's chaos incarnate.

As part of my itinerary, I took the 4WD Safari Tour. The potholed roads made for a bone-jarring journey, with passengers holding on to the open truck's metal frame uprights for dear life. Because the metal can become too hot to touch in the searing heat, they are covered with rolls of black tape. Passengers' hands and sticky black tape resulted in a truckload of tourists doing Al Jolson impressions. Except for me – I was glued fast to the truck's upright. It took a combined effort starting at *Vaihaururu* waterfall to Tahiti's central crater of *Papa I Nia,* to prise me loose with minimum damage.

Any evening on the islands, it is impossible to escape the traditional music, singing, dancing and drumming, laid on for the tourists. The *vahine* wear the traditional, waist-tied *pareos* adorned with grass garland belts and *leis* of tropical flowers, including the national flower, *Tiara Tahiti.* The men dance the Tahitian War Dance holding spears and shields, to the accompaniment of the drums. It is similar to the Maori *Haku,* designed to frighten their enemies. It works for me.

The Tahitian dishes I can recommend include the Mahi-Mahi with shrimp and lobster in white wine; Lagoon fish in vanilla sauce, and Marlin with lobster sauce. Turtles are now protected, but are still eaten by the locals even though to do so is illegal.

The story of 'The Mutiny on the Bounty' is well-known, but, as I have a personal interest in James Cook, the source of Bligh's navigation skills, I decided to take advantage of local history to see what I could find out.

The much maligned Captain Bligh's shipboard discipline was no harsher than on any other ship of the line at that time. After being cast adrift in an open boat, with the loyal members of his crew, Bligh's feat of navigation – in which he trained under James Cook – in reaching East Timor, has never been surpassed. The inquiry, held in London, found Bligh totally exonerated of any blame for the mutiny.

Under secret orders from the Admiralty, Bligh sailed for Tahiti to acquire breadfruit plants – which taste like a combination of bread and potatoes -to be taken to Britain's Colonies as a staple diet for the slaves on the plantations.

What I found, not so widely known, was how close Bligh came to disaster upon his arrival on Tahiti. Upon reaching the beach, Bligh had been greeted by the Chief and his warriors, who asked for news of his friend Captain Cook. Bligh replied that Cook was well, in London, and sent his greetings.

The Chief told Bligh he found that strange, as their brothers to the north, on Hawaii, had sent news some time ago, that they had killed him. Bligh had totally underestimated the Islander's grapevine. How Bligh had talked his way out of a very tense situation must have been a feat comparable to his navigation skills. He got his breadfruit.

Traditionally, when leaving Tahiti, I should have thrown the garland of flowers around my neck into the water. Should it float inshore, towards the lagoon, then I would return to the island; should it float out past the reef and into the open ocean, I was destined never to return. This was a little difficult to determine in my case as I was leaving by air, and they refused to open the door to let me throw it out.

As I needed three pieces, one on each island, my next stop was Bora Bora, 140 miles north-west of Tahiti, 'the most beautiful island in the world', and entirely dependent on tourism. The island is a favourite destination of honeymooners, with the majority of tourists coming from the USA, Japan and Europe, in that order.

Inhabited from the 4th century, James Cook sailed past the island in 1769, and landed there in 1777. True to form, the London Missionary Society moved in, and destroyed the temples in 1820, converted the islanders, and built the first Protestant church.

After landing at Bora Bora airstrip – via Huahine – we were transferred to our hotel by launch. Several resorts have been built on *motus* – small islands – but the first to have overwater bungalows, on stilts over the lagoon, was the Hotel Bora Bora. Now, they are the standard. At the centre of the island are the two main peaks of the extinct volcano: Mount Pahea and Mount Otemana. I first decided to visit 'the capital', the village of Vaitape, on the western side of the island, opposite the lagoon's main channel.

Vaitape boasts a café/bar, a fruit and vegetable stall and a small supermarket. And that is it. I took the ten-minute journey by bus to pick up some wine, only to find it was a religious holiday with no alcohol sales. I really must do more research on some trips. Back to hotel wine list prices. You do have to depend on your resort for your needs.

Although the usual overwater bungalows are available and popular, on Bora bora I prefer a beach bungalow, with its own sun patio and literally one minute from the warm green waters of the lagoon. Bora Bora's lagoon is said to be the best in the world. Snorkelling here is as good as it gets. For scuba divers, there are sharks and rays in deeper water, with organised manta ray and shark-feeding dives.

Our bungalow came with the mandatory Bird of Paradise flower. It is traditional for the turn-down service to place on the bed, one flower for each night of the length of your stay. I know this is meant as a touching gesture, but I get increasingly paranoid as, one by one, the flowers disappear.

Tipping is contrary to the Tahitian code of hospitality. In theory, you are correct not to tip. In reality, it depends how long you are prepared to wait for service. I tip.

It is not widely known that the majority of the island's flora and fauna were originally 'imported'. In addition to 16 varieties of coconut palm, there are over 280 varieties of hibiscus and 37 types of breadfruit. Sweet grapefruit had first been introduced to the island from New Guinea in the 1920s. Explorers, botanists and missionaries had, from 1789, introduced the tamarind tree, the guava from Brazil, the lime and the pineapple. The mango was introduced by a French Admiral. Thanks to an English surgeon named Johnstone, the islands gained the bougainvillea, hibiscus and cacao tree. On the islands, the hibiscus is known as a sailor's purse – 'because it never opens'.

The Polynesians also use certain toxic plants for fishing. Spreading the toxin across the water renders the fish unconscious and easy to catch.

A *motu* is a small islet, and, within a couple of days, we discovered ours: *Moto Rua,* accessed by speedboat and uninhabited. Our very own 'Robinson Crusoe' island. When our boat dropped us off on our *motu,* I gave them a return pick-up time before they left us – I've been caught like that before. Lying on the fine white-sand beach, under the shade of the coconut palms – but not under any coconuts – the tropical rainstorm struck. Across the lagoon, the mountain tops became shrouded in low rainclouds, and the heavens opened. It was torrential, but short.

As the storm passed, we put up our beach umbrella and opened our pre-packed picnic lunch and wine. As we unwrapped the food, a stray black dog, of indeterminate breeding, appeared from nowhere. We ignored it. Suddenly, another dog, of equally indeterminate breeding, appeared and they started copulating, twelve inches in front of our picnic. That, we couldn't ignore. End of picnic due to loss of appetite.

The Bora Bora Lagoonarium is a major marine conservation area, only accessible on a guided tour. We took the tour, on a motorized outrigger, along with twenty other passengers. We began with an en-route stop for snorkelling, then into deep water to feed the Manta Rays and sharks. The feeding of the sharks is safely 'stage managed', with the deployment of a long, buoyed rope for the tourists to grip, as they float face-down in their masks and snorkels. From behind this line of human laundry – or lunch on a rope – the native crew throw pieces of raw fish in front of the line to attract the sharks. The smell of blood in the water attracts a convention of sharks. The sharks dart in, and, showing their crescent of needle-sharp teeth, snatch the fish on the turn, literally only two feet from the watchers. I suggested 'the Nurse' do the feeding, while I took the photos from the safety of the outrigger. As the Americans say: "My momma didn't raise no idiots."

Landing at the Lagoonarium, which involved wading ashore, two of the crew got me ashore by forming a bosun's chair. In the conservation pens, you can snorkel with the Angel and Trigger Fish, rays and turtles. As is now common, I was offered a video or DVD of the day, to be delivered to my hotel later. I declined. I just can't see the motivation for buying a record of twenty people I'll never see again.

I next braved a 4WD journey to the seven-million-year-old volcano – the sacred mountain of the gods – *Oto Maru,* for a panoramic photo shoot. We drove on, down to the lagoon, to see the coconut drying racks on the beach. The small boats suspended on davits, tourists presume this is to avoid damage in case of a repeat of the 1991 hurricane. The fact is more mundane: they are hung simply to avoid them being eaten by termites.

Bora Bora's population of 6,800 is 68% ethnic Polynesian, 20% French (including the police) and 20% Chinese, who are mainly shopkeepers.

Chinese 'coolies' had first arrived as workers for the cane plantations.

In front of the native houses are what tourists presume to be American-style mail boxes, the metal, tunnel-shaped containers on wooden upright posts. In fact, they are the world's most unusual bread bins, with three deliveries a day. On the beach, I gathered some hibiscus flowers and scattered them over a small area. 'The Nurse' waited, poised with the camera. Suddenly, the *Nona Tupa* appeared from their holes in the sand, grasped the hibiscus in their pincers, and disappeared back into their holes carrying lunch. These sand crabs are fed by the locals on papaya and coconut for twelve days, until their flesh turns pink, and they are ready to eat. When visiting native homes, I am always careful as to where I tread in their back gardens. Cremations are illegal, and there are no cemeteries on the island.

The majority of resort hotels provide outrigger canoes for their guests. I suggested we took one out into the lagoon. I had forgotten 'the Nurse's' complete lack of co-ordination or sense of direction. Fifty feet into the lagoon we rammed an overwater bungalow's diving deck. The honeymooners rushed out onto their sun deck above, to check if it was an earthquake. They were very good about it. The husband actually came down to the diving deck and pushed us back out into the lagoon.

We drifted several yards in reverse due to the current, then tried again. We rammed the honeymooner's overwater bungalow for a second time. This time, the husband was not so pleased. As I apologised profusely, I realized the Nurse had been paddling in the opposite direction to myself.

Having ordered the nurse to put her paddle under her seat, I paddled the canoe myself (eventually) back to the shore. The beach staff gave us a round of applause.

My final destination this trip: Moorea, or 'Yellow Lizard', roughly the shape of a heart with two bays. 'The magical island of the Pacific', Moorea is only a fifteen-minute ferry journey from Papeete, and, for us, back to an overwater bungalow.

Although I am usually wary of 'tourist villages', I followed our fellow tourists to Tiki Village: 'Established to preserve the traditional culture and crafts of the island'. In reality, it gives the islanders an opportunity to make a living selling their craftware direct to the tourists. As you watch the local craftsmen working at their stalls, at least you can be sure your souvenirs are genuine. I bought all my small souvenir gifts to take back to the UK at the village. It saved me a substantial amount as opposed to buying them at a shop mark-up; also, I never buy anything for the UK until the end of a trip. Why would I want to carry them round with me on my visit?

We were met at the village by our local Moorean guide for the free tour, including a reconstructed *Marae* – a temple – with its wooden totems and sacrificial stone slabs. Only male children were sacrificed to the gods, which resulted in a problem, obvious even today.

It had been considered an honour to offer up your son for sacrifice. Not all parents agreed. Many boys were concealed from birth, by dressing them as girls, necessity then dictating they were brought up as females for the rest of their lives. I was honestly surprized at the number of transvestites on the islands. Sometimes, it was almost impossible to determine their gender. 'The Nurse' particularly liked a lady with an infectious high-pitched giggle at reception. I had to point out to her 'she' wasn't.

We decided on a traditional lunch at the village, cooked in a ground oven. Food, wrapped in leaves, was placed in a wood and hot stone layered hole in the ground, and left there until ready – which can take several hours. The meat, fish and vegetables were all cooked together in the same oven. Cooking people in the ground oven, has, thankfully, gone out of fashion. Lunch was delicious.

An islander with an outrigger took us out to a black pearl bed. Tuamotu is the only source of genuine black pearls in the world, and extremely expensive. In the underwater cultivation beds, where they are left for three years, the oysters are artificially inseminated to ensure, and limit, the supply of pearls. It is a further two years before the pearls can be exported. Back on shore, the shop has a wide selection of flawless pearl rings, pendants, earrings, bracelets and necklaces, costing five figures and more, depending on the piece. The girl in the shop, showed us a selection through a continuous nasal sniffing. Finally, she excused herself and disappeared into the back of the shop. When she reappeared, her pupils were dilated. 'The Nurse' sympathized with her head cold. I wondered how many lines she was snorting a day.

Several thousand pounds, for me, was not an option. I found an alternative. There were, I was told, a small number of shops and stalls selling flawed, imperfect black pearls at a tenth of the price, depending on their level of imperfection. I did my shopping for 'the Nurse' and friends back in the UK. When they read this, I am in *serious* trouble.

The best way for me to get my bearings on any island, is from its highest point. Back to the Sacred Mountain for a final photo shoot. On my left, lay Cook Bay, and, to my right, Opunohu Bay. In 1777, Cook had sailed from Tahiti and anchored in what is now known as Cook Bay. Mahine, Chief of the Marama, had advised Cook the deeper and safer anchorage would be in the next bay, Opunohu. Mel Gibson's film of 'Mutiny on the Bounty' was filmed in the Bay, known to 'South Pacific' fans as Bali Hai.

'The Nurse' was over-ambitious attempting a climb up to the Coconut Plateau for a photo shoot. It became an evening spectacle to watch the eccentric English couple tackle the steps up to reception. I would limp up one step at a time with my gold-topped cane, then stop. I would then throw the cane back down to 'the Nurse' to repeat the process. This was usually done to a round of applause.

What I inflicted upon myself next is by no means obligatory reading, unless you have serious masochistic tendencies. After a lifetime of 'no distinguishing marks', I decided to acquire tattoos – to 'the Nurse's' horror. I feel it necessary to point out, I do *not* mean tourist tattoos.

With Samuela, a traditional native tattooist, I had to undergo lengthy interrogation to prove my entitlement to several-millennium old traditional designs. The point of tattooing your body – male and female - in the South Pacific, is as a record of your life and your family history. The tattoos can be read as an open book by native islanders. Obviously, mine are Moorean. I asked Samuela when Tahitians considered they had enough tattoos. He gave me a simple answer: "When there is no space left on your body."

When James Cook returned to England with the Tahitian Omai, who had traditional tattoos, he had caused quite a stir. Omai became a celebrity both at Court and in the salons of society; his full-length portrait in white robe and turban, was painted by Sir Joshua Reynolds.

My entitlement having been established, work commenced. The intricate designs were to cover the biceps and shoulders of both arms. This had to be completed in one day. The first tattoo took from 11am to 3pm non-stop. As a warrior, you cannot cry out in pain. 'The Nurse' could bear my silent tears of pain no longer, and absented herself to the sun deck for the duration.

After a short respite to raid the minibar for anaesthetic, the second tattoo took from 7pm to 10pm – a total of seven hours of unrelenting pain. The fact that both male and females had their genitals tattooed, I did not even want to think about.

The first tattoo symbolized the world of water: the ocean, islands and a shark, denoting the rank of tribal chief; the second, an intricate design around a central shark's tooth motif, denoting a warrior.

During the rest of our stay, every local recognized the meaning of the tattoos. One *vahine* even brought her new born baby to see them.

The following morning, I was interviewing the Director General, French Polynesia, of a major resort group, in the football field sized lobby, when he broke off in mid-sentence.

"*Merde!*" He pointed at my left arm.

I was wearing a short-sleeved white shirt. At least, it had been white. Now, it was a blood-soaked red, obviously the aftermath of tattooing. The DG leapt into action. I explained my wife was a nurse. He shouted for a golf trolley "Now!"

Back at the overwater, 'the Nurse' was not amused. She never is in cases of self-inflicted injuries.

The island grapevine kicked in. Whenever we stepped out of our bungalow, we were faced with a golf trolley screeching to an emergency stop, the (always female) staff driver shouting; "Mai Tai?" This is not a cocktail. It is Tahitian for "Are you well?"

The tattoos I now carry are instantly recognisable on any of the islands of the 'golden triangle'. This triangle has its left-hand base in New Zealand, its right on Easter Island, coming to its pointed apex in the Hawaiian Islands. Within the triangle lie the Cook Islands, Fiji, Samoa, the Marquises and others. As it has been for millennia, it is the quickest way of proving your origin and status throughout the South Pacific.

Chapter Twelve
A Stairway Too Far

Memories of previous sojourns to Italy, include my then wife, 'the Model', getting hopelessly lost in the catacombs beneath Rome, and my contracting salmonella poisoning on Capri. My recent visit was to critique the Campania region of south west Italy. Unlike earlier visits, I was now registered as disabled, the problem being mobility, affording me the opportunity to critique from a new viewpoint: disabled friendly or unfriendly.

I had been the victim of a 'travail warning' on this trip, before even leaving the UK. Why don't I listen. A month earlier, I had booked rooms at an airport hotel for the night before our flight, which had been duly taken from my credit card. We checked in.

"I'm sorry, but we have no reservation for you."

"Impossible! I paid for it last month!"

"You paid for a reservation for last month, but are listed here as a no-show."

I had booked the wrong month. As I said to 'the Nurse' and her two friends, "What else could possibly happen?"

I had also booked us into the wrong hotel.

'The Nurse' was not amused.

Our visit began in Naples, home of the Camorra – the Neapolitan Mafia. The Una Hotel, in the Piazza Garibaldi, the centre of Naples, now bears little resemblance to its previous history of the Grand Hotel of Naples. Despite complete refurbishment, its historical glass chandeliers are but a dim and distant memory; one welcome asset is its roof terrace cocktail bar, with its views over the city to Mount Vesuvius and, on this particular evening, providing a grandstand seat for the festival fireworks display. Its main asset remains its location.

To the left of the rooftop terrace were the remaining buildings of the 'old' Naples, and, to the right, the new. Decades earlier, when a major slum clearance project had taken place, its residents had been relocated outside of the city to brand new high-rise apartment blocks. For the first time in their lives, they had modern bathrooms. When the city officials visited to see how they had settled in a little later, they found every bath in the buildings were full of soil, and had been converted into herb gardens. I did, influenced by this, once contemplate filling my shower cubicle with soil and creating a vegetable garden, with the obvious advantage of watering by shower. 'The Nurse' vetoed it, threatening to have me sectioned.

On Sunday morning, I awoke to a cacophony of competing, peeling church bells, heralding the beginning of Saint's Day. In Italy, you can find at least one town or village celebrating their local Saint every day of the year.

From my balcony, two sights I find synonymous with Naples: the week's laundry being brought out to apartment building's balconies and hung to dry on several permanent washing lines suspended from the rails; and the raucous cries floating up from the stalls of the crowded street market in the narrow lanes beneath my window. Jostling through the crowds of shoppers, bartering for a bargain, it became apparent that the stalls making the most money, were those providing false designer label clothing and shoes, fake watches, perfumes and leather ware. On second thoughts, with the fine art of protection and percentage of turnover, the Camorra were probably the ones making the highest profit.

A hectic day: first to the National Archaeological Museum, where I could happily spend a month, particularly in the galleries of busts and statues of the Roman gods, emperors and famous, and the rooms of artefacts from the excavations of Pompeii.

The Catacombs of Naples, in Capo Di Monte, a local bus ride north of the city, are definitely disabled unfriendly. There is no lift, but there is a deep, sloping entrance. Getting down is not a problem, getting back up, impossible. I delegated to 'the Nurse' (again).

In Napoli railway station the next day, I took the advice I had been given not once, but several times: 'On the Circumvesuvio, do not wear a watch or rings, and hide your wallet'. On the 'local trains', the main danger is from pickpockets working in organized groups and not averse to using violence. My downside was my walking cane – it was obvious I would not be able to exactly sprint after them.

The Circumvesuvio is still the cheapest and most efficient way of reaching Sorrento, Pompeii and Herculaneum, both of the latter being buried under the eruption of Mount Vesuvius in 79AD.

Aboard the train – similar to a London Underground carriage – it was standing room only. I was stood by the carriage' sliding doors, when 'the Nurse', and our two travelling companions, several passengers away, saw that I had become the pickpockets' target for today. They could only look on helplessly, as two of the three-man gang, wedged me into the corner. The third reached inside my jacket's inside pocket for my wallet.

Unfortunately for them, my wallet was in its usual place when abroad, in my zipped trouser pocket below my kneecap. Realising their error – now being the proud owners of 'A Tourist's Guide to Sorrento' – they leapt from the train seconds later, at the first station stop. I can only presume they caught the next train returning to Naples, hoping for better pickings.

Known as *Sorrentium* to the Romans, Sorrento remains famous for its locally-produced Limoncella, their alcoholic drink of choice. The lemons grown in this area seem to be twice the size of those grown elsewhere – or maybe that was *after* drinking it.

Taking a taxi from Sorrento Station to our hotel, we climbed up from the peninsular. Reaching a small village square, our driver informed us that, from here, we would have to call the villa to go any further. He pointed to more of an alleyway than a road, disappearing up a steep hill between houses. The road did not look wide enough for a Mini. The Villa shuttle arrived, a milk float posing as a people carrier, but a least it made it up the alley, and logically, doubled as a free shuttle service down to the town.

I had warned Luigi, the head of the family-owned villa, split into apartments, in advance that I had a mobility problem. As we arrived at the villa, I reminded him.

"Si!" he responded with a smile. "You are on the top floor."

I can only manage stairs if they have bannister and landings for rest stops. These did. The climb was more than compensated for by the panoramic view from our balcony over Sorrento to the sea, with Capri and Ischia on the horizon.

The following morning, we took the shuttle into town – or, at least, to the outskirts. The taxis operate a monopoly – hotel shuttles are not allowed to operate from the town centre or the bus and train stations. Sorrento is famous for its intricate wooden marquetry work, from pillboxes to dining tables. 'The Nurse' was looking for a trinket box. I priced them. £95 for a small one. I suggested she get rid of her trinkets.

The social hub of Sorrento is the Piazza Tasso, the central square, and a must for people-watching. All human life is there. Sipping their coffees at the cafés each side of the square, tourists of different nationalities rub shoulders with the locals, moving from one pavement café to the next to follow the sun (tourists) or the shade (locals). However, crossing from one side of the square to the other, do not presume the traffic will stop because you are on a zebra crossing.

The majority of tourists to Sorrento, usually visit the nearby Isle of Capri. Why, I am not quite sure. If Sorrento was good enough for Byron and Keats, it's good enough for me. Before visiting Capri, set a budget. No-one could ever accuse Capri of being cheap. Many years ago, my reason for visiting the Isle was to have lunch or dinner with the entertainer Gracie Fields and her husband in her villa. The first time I met her, I rather tactlessly mentioned my mother had been one of her fans.

She looked me up and down, slowly – then smiled.

"Don't worry about your age, love – I like 'em young."

Gracie was the consummate professional, even in retirement. Beneath her villa, she owned the open-air restaurant by the sea. English tourists, mainly from the cruise ships, were delivered by the coach full. On most days, she would come down to the restaurant, pose for photos with her visitors, and sign autographs. She played up to being a simple, Lancashire lass – but, in reality, she was a shrewd businesswoman.

From Sorrento to Capri, it is quicker to take the *aliscarfe* – the hydrofoil, from the Marina Piccolo. At Capri harbour, the queues for the funicular railway to Capri Town can be horrendous. Once in the town's main square, avoid the bustling crowds, and do a little people-watching over lunch at the Gran Caffé. Capri is, above all, an island for shoppers. Capri's rocky shoreline has only two shingle beaches, but a surfeit of designer shops and boutiques, restaurants and cafés. If taking the bus – again horrendous queueing – to the more elevated town of Anacapri, be prepared for a further plethora of designer labels.

A major tourist attraction is the *Grotto Azzurra* – the Blue Grotto. This sea cave is thought to have been one of the Emperor Tiberius' favourite temples to the Sea Nymphs. As the blue, glowing effect is created by the sunlight entering through an underwater cave mouth, the best time to visit is between noon and 2.00pm. It can be over an hour's waiting time, as the rowing boats queue at the cave's entrance. Once inside, the boatmen will entertain their passengers with Neapolitan songs, whether they can sing or not. Mercifully, the visit to the cave lasts only five minutes.

This time, I had no choice but to delegate. I can no longer visit. To enter the mouth of the cave, passengers must lean backwards into the boat to avoid concussion. Unfortunately, thanks to my compacted vertebrae and a crushed disc, my spine no longer bends in that direction.

As part of my plan was to include a piece on the Claudian Emperors, one of my priorities on Capri was the villa of Tiberius, atop the towering cliffs, and of which very little remains. Should you have read 'I Claudius' by Robert Graves, you have a fairly accurate impression of Tiberius and his reign.

Tiberius took the unprecedented step of relocating his entire court in Rome – and control of the Roman Empire – to Capri, the favourite island of the Emperor Augustus, the founder of the Claudian Dynasty. Before choosing Augustus as his Imperial name, as Octavian he had defeated Mark Antony and Cleopatra in a decisive sea battle, declaring himself Emperor in 27BC.

Tiberius' morals, one could say, left a lot to be desired. He owned the largest collection of pornography in the known world, garnered from every corner of the Roman Empire. He put his collection to good use. His villa hosted the most infamous and excessive orgies. Anyone, male or female, young or old, refusing to participate, was thrown by his Praetorian Guard over the cliff and onto the rocks below.

Leaving Capri was to prove one of those 'survival of the fittest' moments. Problem: it was Republic Day – a major Italian National Holiday. As this evening would be one of family gatherings for the festival and fireworks, the last ferry back to Sorrento was moved to the far earlier time of 4.30pm. The day trippers to Capri, tend to wait for the last ferry to make the most of the island. In this instance, it meant all the tourists who had arrived by several different ferries, were determined to board this final ferry of the day.

As I have travelled a little, I ensured I was sat by its berth with a large Campari and soda. The ferry arrived. The stampede began, running up the boarding ramp and heading for the stairways. I whispered in the ticket collector's ear. He pointed. I duly, as entitled, took the disabled elevator to the top deck for a photo shoot. I was the first one on the top deck.

★ ★ ★ ★

There are two ways to see the Amalfi Drive, carved into the cliffside by the Romans: driving or by sea. Driving is not for the faint-hearted, as the Drive consists of a series of hair-raising blind bends. As it was yet another festival weekend, the whole of the Amalfi Drive was open to two-way traffic. Result: chaos. At every bend where a car met a coach and came to a standstill, it was, given the width of the road and the drop on the seaward side, a case of which driver's nerve broke first. The cacophony of blaring coach and car horns was unbelievable.

The advantage of driving by car, or coach, is flexibility. It enables a visit to the steep cliffside town of Positano, with a choice of which coach to catch on to Amalfi itself. From its promenade on the Drive, Positano is a series of steeply-descending houses and narrow lanes down to the sea. Following lunch at the Positano Bakery on the sloping Via Cristoforo Columbo, and a visit to the mosaic-domed church, I walked, with my cane, down every narrow, shop-crowded lane to the beach and sea. My party consisting of 'the Nurse' and two friends, preferred to climb back up to the Drive, and continue to Amalfi by coach. For me, this was not an option. I must have suffered a mental aberration to have walked down in the first place. Waving them goodbye, I waited on the jetty for the boat to Amalfi.

We had arranged to meet up at one of the tables outside the *Pansa,* opposite the steps up to Amalfi's jewel in the crown: the 9th Century Cathedral of Saint Andrew, a masterpiece of Rococo architecture. Over the centuries, the Cathedral encompassed stunning examples of Romanesque, Byzantine, Gothic and Baroque styles. It dominates the Square, reached by 62 steep steps leading to its medieval bronze doors. A Cathedral has stood on this spot since 596AD.

After two hours of red wine reorders, the rest of the party finally arrived. Evidently, the whole of the Amalfi Drive from Positano to Amalfi was gridlocked, traffic moving only an inch at a time. I waited for them as they looked inside the Cathedral with its off-centre bell tower. They returned and persuaded me to join them on the next coach back to Sorrento. I must have been mad.

We were horrendously late when we finally neared Sorrento. Suddenly, 'the Nurse' and our male friend, leapt to their feet, shouting at the driver to stop.

My question: "Why?"

"We're here! I recognise it! We're just around the corner from Sorrento Railway Station!"

"You're right! We're near the Piazza Tasso!" agreed friend.

We got off the coach. We walked around the corner. It was uncharted territory.

"I don't understand it!"

"I do," I tried to smile. "Remember when you led a Girl's Guide orienteering course, and got lost? Well, congratulations – you've done it again…"

"Where are we?"

"We," I answered, "are in St. Agnello, a suburb of Sorrento."

We went into a Pizza Takeaway and asked them to call a taxi. As you do.

★ ★ ★ ★

For Pompeii, it is better to take the Circumvesuvio train rather than an organised coach tour, enabling you to stay as long as you wish in the excavations. For Mount Vesuvius, there are coaches outside the Pompeii excavations to take tourists on a return journey. As Pompeii is flat, there is no mobility problem as long as you take breaks as necessary. I would not recommend it for wheelchairs, due to its cobbled streets. I was able to walk from the Marina Gate entrance, once leading to the harbour, but now one kilometre inland, to the gladiator training school and arena – the whole length of the city.

Pompeii was still in the process of rebuilding from the devastating earthquake of 63AD, when Vesuvius erupted in 79AD, first raining pumice down on the town, the weight causing the roofs of the buildings to collapse, and turning day into night. Next came the hot ash and, what killed Pompeii's citizens, the surges of hot gas travelling at enormous speed at temperatures of 100°C to 400°C.

The bodies of the citizens, lying as they fell, were hollow under their layer of ash, enabling liquid plaster of Paris to be poured in, as in a mould, providing casts of the corpses at the time of their death. From the Forum, take the once crowded streets to the erotica of the House of the Vetti, with its vivid frescoes and mosaics and beautifully rebuilt garden, and Pompeii's largest house: The House of the Fawn.

I make no apologies for seeking out the brothels. For me, they encapsulate the everyday life of the city through their graffiti. The prostitutes of any Roman town or city are the best sources. Among those in Pompeii, from *'Marcus Clodius Primo was here'*, and *'Artimetus got me pregnant,'* to the more risqué *'Phoebus the perfumer fucks the best'; 'Arphocras had a good fuck here with Drauca for a denarius', 'Virgula to her bloke Tertius – you're a dirty old man!'* and *'Chios, I hope your piles irritate you so they burn like they've never burned before!'*

In theory, all Romans – male or female – had the right to prostitute themselves, or sell the sexual services of their slaves. Statues and wall paintings of Priapus, with his hugely enlarged penis, are found all over Pompeii, but are not considered erotic, rather a symbol of good luck and prosperity and a charm to ward off the 'evil eye'.

The most erotic images and graffiti were taken from the excavations to the 'Secret Cabinet' at the Naples Archaeological Museum and barred from public view.

At the far end of Pompeii is found the gladiatorial school, Olympic-size swimming pool and amphitheatre. It had one entrance for the living, and an exit for the dead; there was dual access stairways for the spectators and tiered seating.

Not all the action was in the arena.

The games could become quite 'heated' when neighbouring towns were in competition. At one such meeting, spectators smuggled weapons into the arena. The subsequent rioting left many dead and injured by the time order could be restored.

The Emperor in Rome imposed a ten-year ban on games in Pompeii.

My personal preference is the better-preserved Herculaneum. Only four miles to the west of Vesuvius, in 79AD it was destroyed before Pompeii. The reason for its better state of preservation is simply that it was buried by boiling mud, to a depth of 75 feet. Amazingly, wood and organic materials survived, including the upper floors of the houses and their timbers, even a wooden partition in the house of the same name.

Herculaneum, unlike the port city of Pompeii, was ostensibly an upmarket Roman holiday resort, then by the sea, with many of its grand villas built by wealthy and important social and political patricians in Campania and from Rome. Now overlooked by the modern town of Resina, the ancient city is reached by a viaduct pathway, being 66 feet higher now than its original site, due to an eruption of Vesuvius in 1631 AD. The entry to Herculaneum is onto the Decumanus Maximus, with its rows of shops and houses, connected by small streets and narrow lanes.

Unlike Pompeii, Herculaneum was not covered in lava, ash, white-hot rocks and lapilli, but by a flow of boiling mud, penetrating every street and building in the city. Some of the populace attempted to escape by sea. Unfortunately, a violent tsunami forced them back to shore, where they took shelter in the boathouses in the marine district, as did citizens in Pompeii. The major difference is that the bodies of the citizens of Herculaneum, which fill every boathouse, are complete skeletons, skulls and bones.

The city's Suburban Baths are the best-preserved of antiquity, with its pillared portico, and the two-storeyed Telephus Relief House being well-preserved also. Even more than Pompeii, it is easy to imagine walking through its busy streets and lanes, rubbing shoulders with its citizens.

If travelling to Herculaneum by train, do *not* get off at Ercolano, but at the next stop: Ercolano Scavi, the excavations. Beware the transits and taxis outside the railway station, touting for passengers – the excavations are within walking distance; however, if mobility challenged, take a taxi, making it clear you will pay when it returns to pick you up. I once made the mistake of asking a driver if he could break a €50 note. Several years later, I am still waiting for my change. It comes as no surprize to me that, it is said, we share half of our DNA with a banana.

Vesuvius last erupted in 1944. The Allied Fleet evacuated 5,000 people from Naples, and had to bring in bulldozers to keep the roads open. Following this eruption, Vesuvius was reclassified as dormant. It is currently estimated that, should Vesuvius again become active, over three million people would be at risk.

★ ★ ★ ★

The Isle of Ischia, some 20 miles from Naples, is renowned for its thermal spas and mud baths, the primary motivation for its 6 million tourists a year. However, I feel I must point out, the Island caters mainly to Germans, many menus being printed in that, now, second language, not entirely surprizing given there are more than 5,000 Germans who are resident on the Island.

Ischia - the Green Island – has, throughout its history, suffered from attacks by Barbary pirates and slavers. In 1544, Barbarossa laid waste to the island, taking over 4,000 men, women and children into captivity, to be sold into slavery. The English composer, Sir William Walton, lived on the island from 1949 to his death in 1983. His villa, *La Mortella,* is famous for its gardens, open to the public.

Unfortunately, I had no pleasant memories of my previous visit to Ischia. The local bus routes cover most of the island, and are the best and cheapest way to see Ischia. I fell afoul of the bus ticketing system. The tickets are only valid between specific times. Uniformed bus inspectors board at random to check all tickets, particularly those of the tourists. An inspector boarded our bus. We smiled, and handed him our tickets. Before our eyes, he transmogrified into Benito Mussolini on a bad day. Screaming at the driver to stop, he literally dragged us off the bus – to the hisses of the local passengers – and marched us to the reception of our Therme Hotel.

Our tickets had expired four minutes before our stop.

At reception, Mussolini informed the duty manager that he was not leaving until we had paid a €100 fine. As the bus inspector did not understand English, I was able to concoct a defence with the duty manager. We both agreed to blame 'the Nurse'.

The duty manager explained to Mussolini that the unintentional offence had occurred due to my wife's lack of an IQ. The manager explained to him that we had bought new tickets for the return journey. Unfortunately, she had thrown the new tickets into a bin, instead of the old ones.

Luckily, my wife does not understand Italian.

Whether the inspector believed this, as he looked at 'the Nurse', who smiled at him sweetly, I have no idea. The duty manager went on to assure the inspector we were VIP guests, and would certainly have our international legal team fight this in court – and bring an action for damages and costs against the bus company. He winked at me. After a tirade of frustration at the duty manager, 'the Nurse' and myself, and the English in general, he stormed out of the hotel.

When we eventually checked-out, I left the duty manager a large tip.

On my most recent trip (in 2016), we took the hydrofoil from Sorrento for the short journey by sea to our hotel, built into the cliffside above its private beach. In theory, the water taxis, similar to rowing boats with an outboard, can be called via the hotel reception. In theory. The problem arises in the evening.

On the small water taxi jetty at Ischia Ponte, we telephoned the water taxi number. The number was not recognised. No problem – we rang the hotel reception. Problem – it wasn't manned late evening. Probably a one-off, we agreed. On the third evening it happened again. Stood in darkness on the Ischia Ponte jetty, we were eventually reduced to jumping up and down (not me with *my* mobility problem), waving our arms wildly and shouting at passing boats; any boats – fishing boats, launches, dirigibles, yachts and ferries – we were desperate. They all waved back – and kept going. After two hours, we were spotted by a water taxi on its way home. Too late, we found the *correct* number for the water taxis on the back of our hotel room door. So much for travel writers.

On the day of our arrival, the water taxi pulled alongside the hotel jetty. I looked up at the hotel. And up, and up and up. And no lift. Not exactly disabled friendly. The hotel's website had mentioned some steps. In fact, I counted 330 feet of steps. Our rooms were at the top of the hotel, with, from our patio, a view of the Cliffside, three feet away.

On the patio, we gathered for a conference. As the hotel restaurant was by the beach, as was the water taxi jetty, we decided I would only climb them, in stages, once down in the morning and once up at the end of our evening. Luckily, halfway up the cliff, was the hotel's reception and a huge, mosaic marble terrace set with tables and chairs, into which I could collapse and take in oxygen. A Sherpa would have been an asset.

All of this faded into insignificance compared to the view from the terrace to the Castello Aragonese. The hotel has possibly the best view on the island. A view to kill for. We headed there.

The Angevin castle atop its high rock island, attached to the mainland by a causeway, had been built over an earlier fortress of 474 BC. In 1301 AD, the erupting of Mount Epomeo had resulted in a settlement within the castle's defences for the safety of the island's citizens, not least from pirate attack. By the end of the 16th Century, the castle's settlement had been home to 1,892 families, the Clarisses Convent, the Abbey of the Basilians from Greece, the Bishop and his Chapter and Seminar and the Prince and the garrison; it also held 13 churches, 5 of which were parishes.

The tunnel entrance has a lift up to the castle for those of us with mobility problems – wheelchairs and the walking wounded – leading to the Church of the Immacolata. From there, further climbing to the summit and battlements is optional. A surfeit of bougainvillea and jasmine-shaded terraces, give 300° panoramic views over to the island, and, seaward, to the Sorrentine Peninsular and the Isle of Capri.

During the visit, I did not draw attention to the fact that, during the Napoleonic War in 1809, the British Navy had bombarded the French-held castle, almost reducing it to rubble.

The castle has been privately owned since 1911, and is also home to a hotel, reputably the most expensive on Ischia.

As we left the castle, crossing the causeway, I noticed more than the usual number of local families and their friends on the promenade, but thought nothing of it.

Mistake.

As darkness fell, after the usual manic flagging down of a water taxi, we disembarked at the hotel jetty. Strangely, the restaurant was in darkness. Then, disaster. The gates to the stairs up to the hotel were padlocked. As the fireworks would later confirm, it was not only Sunday – but another Saint's Day Festival. I was left with only one option: to climb the cliff itself, using what looked like an almost vertical mule track. It almost proved lethal. Finally reaching a side entrance to the hotel terrace, I collapsed.

The following day was 'the Nurse's' birthday. We took the bus to St. Angelo on the coast, and celebrated. The least said about that the better. I came back to the bus in a golf cart.

It was our friend's husband's birthday the next day. To celebrate, we took a bus through the narrow roads to the mountains, and the village of Fontana, with its huge, village square terrace overlooking the sea. The lady-owner of the Bar Epomeo was persuaded to drive us to the foot of Ischia's volcano, Mount Epomeo. As 'climbs R not us', I remained at the foot of the volcano in a bar/ristorante – very quickly realising they only spoke German. Upon 'the Nurse' and friends' return, the husband celebrated his 70th. birthday, having successfully climbed to the white lava topped summit of the volcano. For his return, I had organised a small cake with a candle in it, and a rousing chorus of 'Happy birthday to you', in German.

He hasn't forgiven me yet.

Tanning on the hotel's private beach next morning, 'the Nurse' and friend's husband decided to go for a swim. His wife, reading in a deckchair, looked horrified. With a note of rising panic, she reminded him he was banned from showing his legs in public. Shorts were also embargoed. The Nurse and I were convinced his wife's view of his legs must be a total exaggeration.

It wasn't.

Our unanimous decision was that anything with legs like his should come with a beak.

Being over-confident, I decided to clamber, with walking cane, over the lethal-looking rocks on the beach, some taller than myself. My goal was a restaurant built on stilts over the sea, and usually only accessible by boat. How sensible. Having spotted our group of three, helping the fourth over the rocks, the owner of the 'Pirates' ristorante, clambered over the rocks to help us.

Following a superlative lunch of 'Fruits of the Sea' and local wine, with complimentary doughnuts and liqueur, the owner insisted he take me back to our hotel by boat. Only me. The others had to clamber. Back on our beach, I sat sipping a dry martini. Clambering takes it out of one.

On Ischia, it is mandatory to visit one of the famous thermal spas. We chose the Poseidon Thermal Baths at Forio, at the foot of Mount Epomeo. As I stepped down into the Adriano Pool at 28°C, maximum immersion time 20 minutes, an attendant came running over, shouting. He pointed out we would not be allowed in the pools unless wearing a bathing cap, 'available to buy at the Boutique'.

It was then 'the Nurse' noticed many of the bathers were wearing plastic shower caps. It was also then, that she had her brilliant idea. While waiting for the valid time for our afternoon tickets, we had bought a large bag of fresh cherries at the fruit stall by the entrance. Rummaging in her beach bag, she produced the empty polythene cherry bag and crammed it on my head. The attendant stared, but said nothing. Unfortunately for me, apart from my head, the bag was also full of cherry stones and stalks.

At that moment, our friends arrived, burst into laughter, and took a photo of this new fashion in men's headwear, with me holding up one finger at the camera. I continued my physiotherapy in the 32°C Aphrodite Pool, maximum 15 minutes, and then the 34°C Ischia Pool. As any session should culminate with cold water to increase circulation of the blood, next came the 40°C Apollon Pool for 3 minutes, followed by 15 seconds at 15°C.

After an afternoon at the Poseidon, I felt ready for anything – except, perhaps, the hotel's Himalayas.

We took a water taxi to the narrow streets of shops in Ischia Ponte. As a travel writer, I, of course, arranged the trip to arrive just as all the shops shut for their siesta. The best time to shop is in the evening, when the town comes alive and parties.

Unfortunately, the return ferry to Naples docks at the Commercial Port, not an area to linger in. We dragged our baggage to the nearest bar. We were the only customers. We were soon to find out why.

The waiter arrived, and we asked for the wine list. We didn't get one. The waiter returned with a bottle of red wine, four glasses and bowls of free munchies (which went on the bill). It was then I noticed, lurking in the doorway, the owner, a small woman with a face like a bagful of spanners.

I should have been paying more attention.

I thought 'the nurse' had disappeared on a search for the toilets. Wrong. In fact, she had been marched off by the waiter, on the orders of ferret-face, in search of an ATM – they only accepted cash. When my wife returned, I asked to see the bill. The cost of the bottle of wine was roughly the equivalent to that of a case of excellent claret in the UK. What happened next was unbelievable. In all my years of travelling, it had never happened before. It was a first.

"*Servicio!* My tip! Where is my tip?!"

We sat open-mouthed, until I answered him in Italian.

"Here's your tip: stop ripping off the tourists – asshole!"

★ ★ ★ ★

The infamous photo of my cherry bag head-wear, and my photo of friend's husband's legs, we thought we had covered under a 'no-show' gentlemen's agreement.

We failed to take into consideration that our wives are not gentlemen.

The photos are currently in circulation – particularly at parties.

Now, I'm afraid, you will have to excuse me. I have to pack.

Reprint of # - CO - 197/132/16 - CB - Lamination Gloss - Printed on 21-Mar-17 19:35

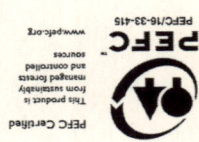

MIX

Paper from
responsible sources

FSC
www.fsc.org

FSC® C004959

PEFC Certified

This product is
from sustainably
managed forests
and controlled
sources

www.pefc.org

PEFC

PEFC/16-33-415

An environmentally friendly book printed and bound in England by www.printondemand-worldwide.com

9 781784 564544